Experiencing Dance

From Student to Dance Artist

Helene Scheff, RDE

Marty Sprague, MA

Susan McGreevy-Nichols

Human Kinetics

Library of Congress Cataloging-in-Publication Data

Scheff, Helene, 1939-
    Experiencing dance : from student to dance artist / Helene Scheff,
Marty Sprague, Susan McGreevy-Nichols.
        p. cm.
Includes bibliographical references.
    ISBN 0-7360-5187-2 (soft cover)
    1. Dance--Vocational guidance. I. Sprague, Marty, 1950- II.
McGreevy-Nichols, Susan, 1952- III. Title.
    GV1597.S33 2004
793.3'023--dc22

                            2003023848

ISBN: 0-7360-5187-2

The Web addresses cited in this text were current as of January 2004, unless otherwise noted.

Acquisitions Editor: Judy Patterson Wright, PhD; **Developmental Editor:** Amy Stahl; **Assistant Editors:** Amanda Gunn, Bethany Bentley, Cory Weber; **Copyeditor:** Jan Feeney; **Proofreader:** Alisha Jeddeloh; **Permission Manager:** Dalene Reeder; **Graphic Designer:** Nancy Rasmus; **Graphic Artist:** Kathleen Boudreau-Fuoss; **Photo Managers:** Kareema McLendon and Kelly Huff; **Cover Designer:** Andrea Souflée; **Photographer (interior):** Photos provided courtesy of Helene Scheff and Marty Sprague, unless otherwise noted; **Art Manager:** Kelly Hendren; **Illustrators:** Tim Offenstein, Argosy (pp. 5b, 5d, 9, 10c, 16), Keith Blomberg (p. 5c), Katherine Galasyn-Wright (pp. 5a, 10a, 10b, 11d, 11e), Mic Greenberg (pp. 6, 9a, 9b); **Printer:** United Graphics

Printed in the United States of America   10   9   8   7   6   5   4   3   2   1

Human Kinetics
Web site: www.HumanKinetics.com

United States: Human Kinetics
P.O. Box 5076, Champaign, IL 61825-5076
800-747-4457
e-mail: humank@hkusa.com

Canada: Human Kinetics
475 Devonshire Road Unit 100, Windsor, ON N8Y 2L5
800-465-7301 (in Canada only)
e-mail: orders@hkcanada.com

Europe: Human Kinetics
107 Bradford Road, Stanningley, Leeds LS28 6AT, United Kingdom
+44 (0) 113 255 5665
e-mail: hk@hkeurope.com

Australia: Human Kinetics, 57A Price Avenue, Lower Mitcham, South Australia 5062
08 8277 1555
e-mail: liaw@hkaustralia.com

New Zealand: Human Kinetics
Division of Sports Distributors NZ Ltd.
P.O. Box 300 226 Albany
North Shore City, Aukland
0064 9 448 1207
e-mail: blairc@hknewz.com

►►► CONTENTS

►►► ACKNOWLEDGMENTS

Just as dancers receive support and guidance from many people in their process of becoming dancers, authors receive guidance and support from many people in their process of writing and publishing a book. Over the years we have had many teachers, mentors, and colleagues that helped shape us into the dancers and dance educators that we are today. In the writing of this book, we have many people to thank: Dr. Edward Scheff, Jordan Scheff, Daniel Scheff, Karen Mellor, all our students over the years, participants at professional development seminars and workshops, and other educators that voiced the need for their students to have a textbook such as this. We thank our colleagues who gave us permission to use photos and information that we pass on to you. Dance is a living, breathing legacy that needs to be nurtured. As we pass this legacy along to you, we also look back and thank the dance educators over the years who have passed their legacy on to us.

These acknowledgments would not be complete without a reverence (a dancer's bow) to the people at Human Kinetics for their vision of this book. We especially thank Judy Wright and Amy Stahl, who guided us through the process. We were very fortunate to have worked with them.

►►► HOW TO USE THIS BOOK

Since before you were born, you were communicating through movement. A well-placed kick told your mother, "I am here!" After birth, you quickly learned how to use your body language as well as your voice to communicate your needs. As a toddler and young child, you spun until you fell down dizzy, danced to music, and continuously improved your movement skills. Do you remember when you were first successful at skipping, shooting a basketball, or jumping rope? Why should this joy in physical movement stop as you mature?

In school, learning is often carried out with words. Imagine learning a fun way to communicate what you know without words. Imagine meeting educational standards, learning about good teamwork, practicing effective learning strategies, and demonstrating improved physical skills while starring in your own dance production!

You are about to embark on a special journey through the world of dance. You will experience dance firsthand. The 15 chapters in this book take you to places you may have been before, but through this journey you will begin to appreciate what goes into the making of a dance artist.

Have you ever taken a train trip where the train stopped at different stations and you could spend a different amount of time at each place? Learning by participating in the activities in this book is very much the same adventure. Whether you go through this book chapter by chapter in sequence or skip around, you will find useful learning experiences each step of the way.

Experiencing Dance is divided into five parts: What Is Your Movement Potential?; Movement Everywhere, But Is It Dance?; How to Become a Choreographer; How to Become a Dancer; and How to Refine Yourself As a Dance Artist. Each part addresses a different aspect of your dance education. Look at the titles of the parts, then decide which part is most interesting and important to your training.

Each chapter within a part has at least three lessons that take you through the subject matter. Icons establish which part of the chapter or lesson you will address. Each chapter begins with an Overture—a short piece on a subject related to the topic of the chapter. At the beginning of each chapter, goals and contents are outlined. If you are self-directed, these items will help you determine which of the chapters you would like to tackle first. If you are teacher-directed, the page will help you know what is expected of you. In either case, you will find review questions at the end of each chapter, including true and false, matching, short-answer, and essay questions.

Each lesson is divided into the following sections:

5,6,7,8 Move It!

This lesson section is in the form of a task that gets you moving and thinking about the topic with only your prior knowledge as a basis for the work.

Vocabulary

This lesson section lists terms that may be new to the reader and are defined in the text.

Curtain Up

This lesson section is where you get information about the lesson's topic.

 ## Take the Stage

This lesson section gives you a task that applies the knowledge you have gained from Curtain Up.

 ## Take a Bow

This lesson section is designed to evaluate your understanding of Curtain Up and your work from the Take the Stage.

 ## Spotlight

This lesson section acquaints you with a person, thing, event, or place aligned with the topic.

Did You Know?

This lesson section brings you a tidbit of information that will add to your overall knowledge of the topic.

With each lesson using the same format as the others, your trip through this dance experience will be easier. Many travelers on a trip keep a diary of their adventures. You should do the same, by keeping a personal journal that will act as a remembrance of your dance experience. Your journal could include the following:

- Reflections on your work (work is the result of any sort of activity or task you do; most of the student work will be part of Take the Stage and Take a Bow)
- Thought processes and feelings
- Observations
- Notes on lessons, skills, and concepts learned

This personal journal could become part of your ongoing portfolio or collection of work. Your portfolio may consist of your journal, student work, documentation of projects, résumé, and anything else that would indicate your familiarity and proficiency within the dance world. (Chapter 15 addresses portfolio, résumés, and marketing yourself.)

The most important thing is to catch the excitement of this journey, figure out what more you might like to know about a particular subject, and then go for it! We hope that you do catch this excitement and remain dance-happy for the rest of your life . . . if not as a dancer then as a dance advocate, dance audience, and dance enthusiast.

Surveying Your Instrument: Body at Work

1

▶▶▶▶▶▶▶▶▶▶▶▶▶▶▶▶▶▶▶▶▶▶▶▶ ▶▶▶▶▶▶▶▶▶▶▶▶▶▶▶▶▶▶▶▶

▶▶▶▶▶▶▶▶▶▶▶▶▶▶▶▶▶▶▶▶

From chapter 1 you will

1. be able to explain what healthy, vertical alignment is and demonstrate your own vertical alignment;

2. know what the major bones, muscles, and joints are and how they interact to make you move;

3. be able to create a dance phrase based on your knowledge of types of joints and the types of movement possible at each joint; and

4. be able to take a personal survey of your body, noting its strong points and limitations.

►Overture

I'm feeling well tuned.

Have you ever thought of your body as an instrument? A musician takes very good care of his instrument, recognizing both its strengths and limitations. When you dance, just as when you play sports, your body is your instrument. Taking care of your instrument and knowing its strengths and limitations will help you gain confidence in your abilities and help you determine what dance forms suit your instrument. You wouldn't play classical music on an old player piano. Neither would you play hard rock on a piccolo. The sound would not be right. In much the same way, your body may be more suited to one dance form than to another. But, before you can know this, you have to know about bones, muscles, and joints.

►LESSON 1.1

Stand on Your Own Two Feet

5,6,7,8 Move It!

Tuck your hips under, push them forward, and tighten your buttocks muscles. Now try to walk. How does this feel to you? Lift your abdominal muscles up toward your rib cage. You will notice that your buttocks can now relax. Again, try walking. How does the walk feel to you now? What do you think makes the difference?

Vocabulary

alignment • kyphosis-lordosis • lordosis • over-muscling • port de corps • tour en l'air • demi-plié • anterior iliac superior

Curtain Up

Physics and gravity dictate that for every job there is a most efficient posture, one that will give the mover power and control. When you pick up a heavy package, you can do a better job and protect yourself from injury if you bend your knees, keep your hips under you, and use your legs to lift the weight. Likewise, when you do a port de corps back (high release or back bend), you will be able to go farther into the backspace if you start with a neutral, supported lower back. If your lower back is already in a sway back position (the pelvis is tipped forward), your spine is already curved, which will limit how far into the backspace you can go with the upper spine.

One of the functions of the skeleton is to provide support and structure. A teacher once told students to "stack their bones" in order to stand in vertical alignment with ease and to just "move their bones" when dancing. The best dancers make the difficult seem easy. A dancer will last longer in the short run (during an ener-

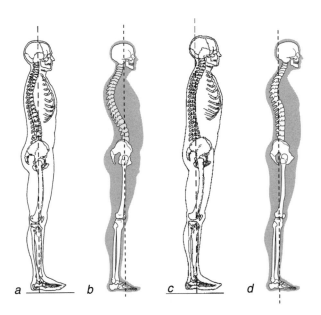

► Skeletal alignment: *(a)* ideal vertical alignment, *(b)* kyphosis-lordosis posture (the spine has an exaggerated "S" shape when viewed from the side), *(c)* flat-back posture, *(d)* lordosis (swayback) posture.

(a) Reprinted, by permission, from L.A. Cartwright and W.A. Pitney, 1999, *Athletic training for student assistants* (Champaign, IL: Human Kinetics), 97; (b and d) From P.A. Houglum, 2001, *Therapeutic exercise for athletic injuries: Athletic training education series* (Champaign, IL: Human Kinetics), 346, (c) From J.C. Griffin, 1998, *Client-centered musculoskeletal assessment* (Champaign, IL: Human Kinetics), 64.

getic dance) and in the long run (throughout a career) if she can move with the least amount of effort. Overmuscling a movement, or straining, is not attractive and could be damaging. One of the reasons a dancer overmuscles a movement is that she does not use good alignment. Alignment is proper, healthy, functional posture. More muscle energy is required when the body is not aligned correctly. A beautiful 360-degree tour en l'air (a turn in the air) is not easily started or completed without a proper demi-plié (a bend of the knees with the knees aligned over your toes). Also important is to have the skull, rib cage, and pelvis stacked evenly during the preparation, the jump, and the landing.

Injuries can occur when a dancer does not use proper alignment. The body is not stupid. If body parts are not stacked atop one another, the body will automatically work to keep from falling over. Muscles will tighten to hold the improper posture. This tensing of muscles could cause soreness or injury. A spine with either too much or too little curvature is in danger of being damaged. Ankle and knee injuries can occur when the knees are not aligned over the toes. Efficient body mechanics require proper alignment; and, just as an engine needs a tune-up, so does a dancer's body. Every so often, a dancer should take some time to check out and correct alignment.

 Take the Stage

As you learn about correct alignment you will want to make sure that you can achieve it yourself. By going through the following process, you will be on the right track.

1. Look at the four types of alignment (postures) in the Curtain Up illustrations. Try copying each, making sure that you look carefully at where the bones are in relation to a vertical line. For instance, in the swayback posture, lordosis (posture D), the head is thrust forward, the pelvis is tilted back, the hip joints are thrust forward, and the knees are jammed back. Lordosis is in the lower spine. Kyphosis is in the upper spine. Kyphosis-lordosis is misalignment in both the upper and lower segments of the spine.

2. Now try walking in each position. In which position are you looking straight ahead and swinging your arms and legs easily? You are right if you said posture A, which is the healthy vertical alignment.

3. To make certain you can establish and maintain your vertical alignment, look at where the vertical line runs in posture A. It runs just behind the ear lobe, the center of the shoulder joint, the anterior iliac superior spine (the front part of the pelvis, which we often hit on counters), the knee joint, and finally just in front of the outside ankle bone.

4. Another way to establish vertical alignment is to imagine circles around the skull, shoulders, hips, and ankles (see the illustrations on page 6). The midpoints of the circles should all line up.

5 Try using this image and the one in this lesson's Curtain Up. Which one works best for you?

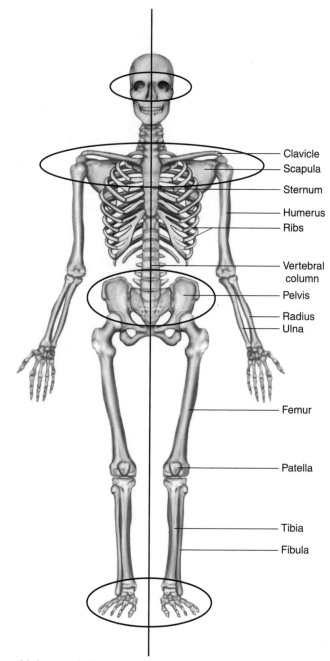

► A mental image to help establish vertical alignment.

Adapted, by permission, from T.R. Baechle and R.W. Earle, 2000, *Essentials of strength training and conditioning*, 2nd edition (Champaign, IL: Human Kinetics), 27.

 Take a Bow

In small increments you will be able to assess your ability to achieve correct alignment.

1. Do a demi-plié, then straighten and do a relevé without losing your vertical alignment. Use a mirror or ask a partner to critique your alignment in this exercise.

Try this in parallel first and second positions and in turned-out first and second positions.

2. Ask a partner to critique your alignment while you jump and then while you do a tour en l'air. Use these comments to improve your jumps and turns.

3. In a journal, write about any changes you have made to improve your alignment. You may keep a journal in which you write (1) reflections on your work; (2) thought processes and feelings; (3) observations; and (4) notes on lessons, skills, and concepts learned. This journal may also become part of your portfolio, which is an ongoing collection of your work.

Spotlight: Lulu Sweigard

Lulu Sweigard (1895-1974) thought of using the imagination to enhance alignment and movement potential. Although she was not the first, she was responsible for organizing the works of her teacher, Mabel Todd. Todd used imagery as a teaching tool, and Sweigard organized and created new visualizations in the teaching of dance and postural alignment. All this took place in the mid-1920s and into the early 1930s. Two good resources for this subject are *Dynamic Alignment Through Imagery* and *Dance Imagery for Technique and Performance,* both by Eric Franklin (Human Kinetics 1996; 1996).

Did You Know? Cross-Training

There was a time when ballet dancers were *not* permitted to take a modern dance class, and conversely, modern dancers weren't permitted to take ballet. It was similar thinking that kept dancers from taking part in sports competition and training and, of course, kept athletes from taking dance classes. In the 1950s Robert Joffrey (1930-1988) and Gerald Arpino (1928-) danced with the May O'Donnell dance company doing modern dance, though they were trained in ballet. (They were also involved in creating ballets for the very early Joffrey Ballet.) New York City's High School of Performing Arts had their dance students taking both ballet and modern (with guest teachers occasionally teaching jazz and ethnic dance forms), and the instructors found that the ballet majors had much to learn from studying modern, and the modern majors had much to learn from studying ballet.

About the same time, athletic coaches were looking at the way dancers trained, and they thought that their athletes would sustain fewer injuries if they used dance warm-ups in their training. The also recognized that dancers were very fast on their feet and could make very quick changes in direction. Hence baseball, football, and basketball players began thinking about the athleticism of dancers. Lynn Swann took ballet classes and says that he owes his football career to the work he did in ballet. All this cross-training leads to good alignment, efficient use of muscles, and protection of bones.

Body Mechanics: Matching Movement to Muscles and Bones

5,6,7,8 Move It!

Repeat the illustrated simple jazz arm exercise until your muscles get tired. In this way you will be able to identify which muscles are doing the work in this exercise.

With a partner, take turns doing a similar movement with resistance. (Refer to the following illustrations.) Note: One person does movement while the other person presses or pulls on the body part in the opposite direction (resistance).

With your partner, discuss which muscles you felt when you bent your elbow (flexion) and when you straightened your elbow (extension).

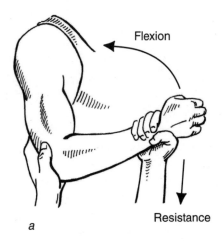

► Do this jazz arm exercise until your arms get tired.

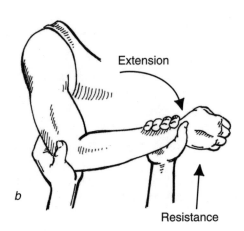

► How to provide resistance to (a) flexion and (b) extension of the elbow joint.

 ## Vocabulary

synovial joint • ligament • tendon • prime mover • antagonist • concentric contraction • eccentric contraction • synergist • fixator • kinesiologist

Curtain Up

The skeletal system has three major functions. It gives your body support and form. The bones and their attached muscles determine the body's structure. The skeleton provides protection for internal organs. Consider what vital organs your skull (brain), rib cage (lungs and heart), and pelvis (reproductive organs) house and protect. The skeletal system also allows for movement. Bones play a passive role in movement, but their shapes, lengths, and places where muscles can attach dictate how the body moves.

Joints are where two bones meet. Movement occurs at the joints. Although there are various types of joints, dancers, athletes, and kinesiologists (those who study the principles of mechanics and anatomy in relation to human movement) are usually concerned with synovial joints. Synovial joints (such as the knee) include cartilage-covered bone endings (a form of connective tissue that is smooth and elastic), a capsule (also made up of connective tissue) that protects and strengthens the joints and syno-

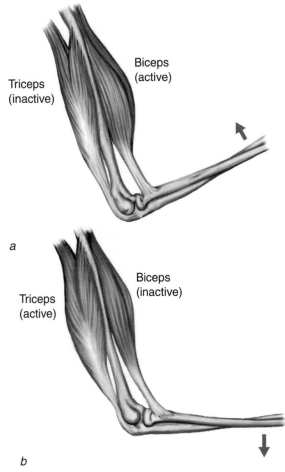

a

b

► Concentric and eccentric contractions. *(a)* Flexion of elbow: biceps do a concentric contraction while triceps do an eccentric contraction. *(b)* Extension of elbow: biceps do eccentric contraction while triceps do concrentric contraction.

Reprinted, by permission, from T.R. Baechle and R.W. Earle, 2000, *Essentials of strength training and conditioning*, 2nd edition (Champaign, IL: Human Kinetics), 26.

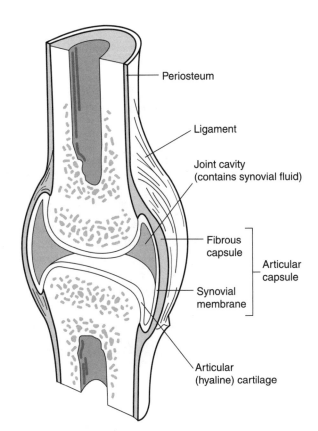

► Cut-away illustration of a synovial joint.

Reprinted, by permission, from R.S. Behnke, 2001, *Kinetic anatomy* (Champaign, IL: Human Kinetics), 10.

vial fluid that lubricates the joint (like oil in an engine). Ligaments (tissues that connect bones to bones) and muscles also strengthen and protect the joints. The freedom and direction of movement possible at a joint are determined by how the ligaments are placed and the shape of the bone endings.

The muscular system contains muscles, tendons (which connect the muscles to the bones), and ligaments. The muscles actively work to produce movement. Simply put, the muscles shorten and lengthen while pulling on the bones, thereby creating motion. During a movement, one muscle shortens.

This muscle is called the prime mover (a muscle that is mainly responsible for a motion). On the other side of the bone, its antagonist (a muscle that counteracts, or slows down a motion) lengthens in opposition. In this way, not only is movement created, but also the joints are protected from too sudden or too much force. For example, in the Move It! exercise the following occurred: To bend (flex) your elbow, the biceps did a shortening (concentric) contraction while the triceps did a lengthening (eccentric) contraction. In extending your elbow, the muscle groups reverse roles.

Note here that the previous explanation is extremely simplified. Kinesiologists and physical trainers dedicate long hours of study and research to understand how movement is created by the skeletal and muscular systems. Other muscles, called synergists, often help the prime movers. Also, fixators (muscles that hold or fix a body part in a particular position to support the movement of another body part) hold other body parts in place so that a certain motion can be done efficiently.

 # Take the Stage

The following exercise is a matching game for linking muscles and joints.

1. Identify the two sets of muscles that are the prime movers and antagonists for the following joints in the illustrations on pages 10-11: shoulders, wrists, fingers, hips, knees, and ankles.

2. Write your predictions or guesses next to the name of the joint.

3. While moving the joint, touch the muscles to see if your predictions are true. Make any needed corrections. Use the partner work that you did in lesson 1.2 Move It! to help you with your work. (Remember how your partner provided careful resistance.)

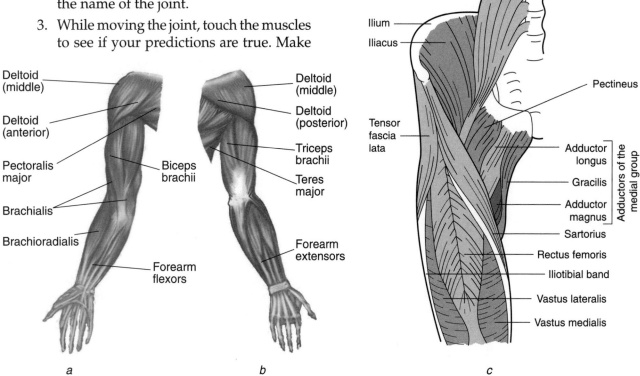

► Muscles of the arms and legs: (a) anterior view of arm and shoulder; (b) posterior view of arm and shoulder; (c) anterior view of hip.

a and b: Adapted, by permission, from T.R. Baechle and R.W. Earle, 2000, *Essentials of strength training and conditioning*, 2nd edition (Champaign, IL: Human Kinetics), 29.

c: From J.E. Donnelly, 1990, *Living anatomy*, 2nd edition (Champaign, IL: Human Kinetics), 143. Adapted by permission of author.

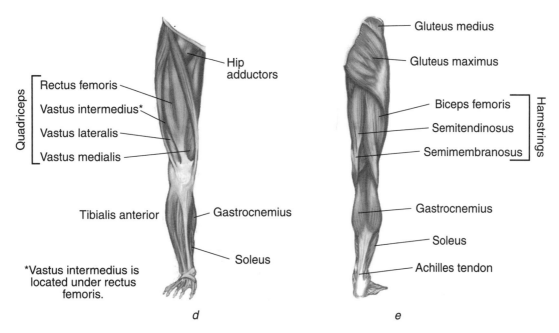

► Muscles of the legs: (d) anterior view of leg; and (e) posterior view of leg.

Adapted, by permission, from T.R. Baechle and R.W. Earle, 2000, *Essentials of strength training and conditioning*, 2nd edition (Champaign, IL: Human Kinetics), 29.

 Take a Bow

Compare your work with another student's work. It would be preferable if this student were not your first partner. Discuss and defend your findings. Make any needed corrections on your prediction list.

1. Check your results with your teacher.
2. Make corrections on your prediction list as needed.

 Spotlight: Irene Dowd

Irene Dowd (1946-) studied with and assisted Dr. Lulu Sweigard at the Juilliard School from 1968 through 1974. Irene performed under the direction of Anna Sokolow and José Limón at the Juilliard School and has choreoraphed extensively for her own company and others. Currently, she is on the faculty at the Juilliard School and the National Ballet School of Canada. She choreographs regularly for solo dancers, including Peggy Baker and Margie Gillis. She has a BA in philosophy from Vassar College, and studied anatomy and neuroanatomy at Columbia Presbyterian Medical School and neuroscience at Teachers College, Columbia University. In the third edition of her book, *Taking Root To Fly,* Ms. Dowd speaks of the process of seeing and touching her students as they go through movements in daily activities.

Did You Know? Gray's Anatomy

Many resources can help you learn more about the human anatomy. One of the most popular is *Gray's Anatomy of the Human Body*, by Henry Gray (1825-1861). In 1858, the first English edition of *Gray's Anatomy* was published. Now in its 30th edition, it still serves as a primer for students of anatomy worldwide. You can visit your local library or bookstore to check out this valuable resource. For an interesting alternative, try using the *Gray's Anatomy Coloring Book*.

Dancing at the Joint

Adapted, with permission, from S. McGreevy-Nichols, H. Scheff, and M. Sprague, 2001, *Building more dances: Blueprints for putting movements together*, Champaign, IL: Human Kinetics, pp. 75–77.

5,6,7,8 Move It!

Do a joint survey warm-up by exploring all the movements possible at each joint. Try to move only one body part at a time (isolations). While moving, pay attention to what type of movement is possible at each joint, how free and large this movement can feel (range of motion), and which joints can do similar movements as others. To start, follow the instructions for head (neck) and shoulder joint isolations.

1. Starting with the neck in neutral position, move your head down to your chest, then straighten back to neutral. Move your head back by stretching your nose toward the ceiling, and return to neutral. Turn your head right and left, and return to neutral. Tip your head sideways to the right and left, and return to neutral. Slide your chin forward and backward, and return to neutral.

2. Lift your shoulders up and press them down; slide them forward and backward. Roll the arms inward toward your chest. Then roll the arms backward toward your spine. Circle the shoulders backward, and forward.

Continue down the body, exploring movement at each of the major joints.

Vocabulary

isolation • range of motion (or movement) • **rubric** • **types of joints:** pivot • gliding • ball and socket • hinge • ellipsoid • saddle • **types of movements:** flexion • extension • hyperextension • elevation • depression • inward rotation • outward rotation • circumduction • adduction • abduction • inversion • eversion

Curtain Up

Dancers need to be aware of all movements that their bodies can produce. They should know what kinds of movements and what ranges of motion are possible at each of their joints. It's important to understand what is anatomically possible not only for the human body but also for each individual body. All people are put together in unique ways. Every dancer's instrument (body) has different capabilities and talents. Two people doing the same dance step could look completely different because they are put together differently and have different ways of moving. It is a healthier approach to invest effort and time in developing and improving on what your body can do rather than forcing it to copy another dancer. One dancer should not be compared to another.

The types of joints are

- pivot (top of neck),
- gliding (wrist),
- ball and socket (hip),
- hinge (knee),
- ellipsoid (wrist), and
- saddle (thumb).

These joints are all synovial joints, as discussed in lesson 1.2. Examples of where these types of joints occur are listed in parentheses, but there are other places in the body where these joints are also found.

Types of movement that can be done at these joints include

- flexion (bending, or decreasing the angle between two bones),
- extension (straightening, or increasing the angle between two bones),
- hyperextension (going beyond straightening),
- elevation (lifting),
- depression (pressing downward),
- inward rotation (turning in),
- outward rotation (turning out),
- circumduction (combination of flexion, extension, adduction, and abduction; this seems like full circling),
- adduction (moving toward the midline of the body),
- abduction (moving away from the midline of the body),
- inversion (sideways movement sliding inward), and
- eversion (sideways movement sliding outward).

These different types of movements are possible in different types of joints. For example, flexion and extension are possible at the hinge joint of the knee.

Take the Stage

It is helpful to know what movements your joints are capable of doing. Then you'll know what conventional, as well as unconventional, movements you can expect of your joints.

1. Identify other examples of joints that are like the types of joints listed in the Curtain Up text. For example, the knee is similar to the elbow. Both are hinge joints, and flexion and extension are the types of movement possible there.

2. Review the Move It! activity in lesson 1.3 and identify both the types of joints used and the types of movement that can be done at each joint. Write your answers in your journal or on a piece of paper. Also note when the movement in a particular joint feels restricted (not done with ease). Write down these discoveries.

3. Create an isolation dance phrase from movement discovered in the previous movement activities. While dancing, name out loud the types of joints and movements that you are using in this dance phrase. Have your dance phrase videotaped.

Spotlight: Bill Evans

Adapted, with permission, from Bill Evans, www.billevansdance.org/bio.htm.

Bill Evans (1940-) is a dancer, teacher, choreographer, lecturer, administrator, movement analyst, and writer with a uniquely varied and comprehensive background of experiences and accomplishments. He is a full professor and former head of dance in the department of theatre and dance, College of Fine Arts, University of New Mexico at Albuquerque, where he joined the faculty in 1988. He is artistic director of the Bill Evans Dance Company (founded in 1975) and also director of the Bill Evans Summer Institute of Dance (founded in 1976) and the Bill Evans Teachers' Intensives (founded in 1999). Professor Evans maintains an active career as a freelance choreographer and solo performer and has appeared in all 50 states as well as Australia, Canada, England, Finland, France, Germany, Hungary, India, Ireland, Italy, Japan, Mexico, New Zealand, Norway, and Russia.

Professor Evans has created and is continually refining a theory and technique of training dancers, which is notable for its integration of concepts from Laban and Bartenieff Movement Analysis, body correctives, and applied kinesiology. This technique has been taught in workshops and college and university dance departments throughout North America and Europe. Its focus is on developing a balance of mobility and stability and of stretch and strength, while fully understanding and utilizing the body–mind potential in a regenerative way of moving and thinking, which extends the dancer's career and enjoyment of his or her ability to experience full access to three-dimensional space and a full qualitative range of expression.

► Bill Evans.

Photo courtesy of Pat Berrett.

Take a Bow

Go through the following assessment process to determine how the knowledge you gained applies to your dance phrase.

1. After viewing your dance phrase, evaluate whether you performed your isolation dance with clear, pure movements and whether you named the types of joints and movements correctly.

2. In your journal, identify at least three improvements that you could make in your dance phrase. Revise your dance phrase by making these improvements.

3. With a partner, review and discuss all of the information from items 1 and 2 in this process.

4. If your teacher provides a rubric, use it to evaluate your work in this lesson. A rubric is a list of items that should be included in your work; each item also assigns a score to your work.

5. After completing lesson 1.3 Take the Stage, create a short dance using only one or two types of movement. For instance, you could create this dance using only flexion and extension. Share this dance with your class.

Did You Know? Kinesiology

Kinesiology is the study of the principles of mechanics and anatomy in relation to human movement. The field of kinesiology, which has expanded to include the areas of dance medicine and science, has helped identify many of the physical problems related to dancing. To find out more about these topics and other related areas, conduct a Web search using any of these key words: "dance medicine and science," "injury prevention," "somatic science," "Feldenkrais Method," "dance therapy," "mind/body arts and sciences," "Alexander Technique," and "Pilates." You can also contact the International Association of Dance Medicine and Science (IADMS) for more information about the field.

Personal Physical Survey

5,6,7,8 **Move It!**

Before doing this activity, attend a dance class. This can be a dance class in your school or anywhere else. Pay attention to movements that feel restricted, small, or tight. Note in which areas of the body (joints or muscles) these restrictions take place. Also note when movements feel free and can be done with ease. Note in which areas of the body (joints or muscles) these easy movements take place. Write these observations in your journal.

Vocabulary

hyperextended knees

Curtain Up

Dancers, like athletes, appear to never be satisfied with their bodies' capabilities. They are always pushing themselves to be better. A dancer's goal is to have a body that is capable of doing anything that a piece of choreography could require. Dance training involves work that both strengthens weak areas and stretches tight areas of the body. A dancer seeks to develop a powerful yet fluid body.

In reality, few people have the perfect body. The best approach to an effective training program is first to assess the body's abilities and limitations. During your dance training and the first three activities in this book, you may have noticed that the range of motion in some joints seems limited. Sometimes limits in range of motion are caused by the makeup of your skeleton (structure of bones), and there is nothing you can do but accept this limitation and work around it. Sometimes this physical trait is due to muscle functioning and can be improved with training. Of course, each dancer has uniquely amazing abilities and loves doing movements that accentuate those abilities.

Take the Stage

Knowing your own body and its limitations is helpful to your creative process. You won't want to use movements that are beyond your range of motion. You can refer to your journal to review your thoughts on the following concepts.

1. Look at your journal entry for lesson 1.3. Which joints seemed limited in their range of motion? Which joints allowed for free and full range of motion?

2. Look at a video of yourself in a technique class or performance. Write in your journal your observations of what parts of your body seem to function well and what parts seem limited in their range of motion. If you do not have a video of yourself, you can ask your teachers or fellow dancers to tell you their observations, or remember the dance class in which you observed your own abilities and limitations for this lesson's Move It! section.

3. Using the following illustrations, the teacher's handout, or your own drawing of a body, place a plus (+) on the parts of the body that you think function well, and place a minus (–) on the parts that you think may be limited in function.

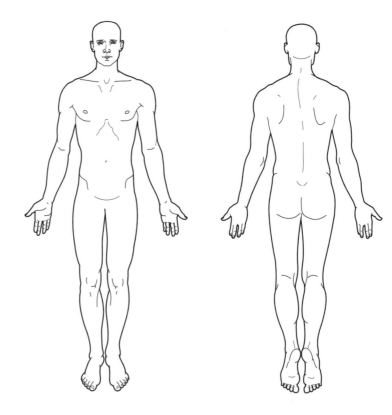

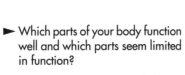
► Which parts of your body function well and which parts seem limited in function?

Reprinted, by permission, from S.J. Shultz, P.A. Houglum, and D.H. Perrin, 2000, *Assessment of athletic injuries: Athletic training education series* (Champaign, IL: Human Kinetics), 46.

Take a Bow

To check your objectivity, share your observations with your peers and teachers, and discuss their observations of your body's abilities. This activity's learning can be used as a basis for directing your future personal dance training. Write a short essay stating your goals and an action plan for your future personal dance training.

Spotlight: Joseph Pilates

Joseph H. Pilates (1880-1967), a German-born boxer and circus performer, developed a series of exercises and spring-resisted equipment while interned in English camps during World War I. He had suffered from asthma and rheumatic fever and was determined that he and his fellow prisoners would come out of the camp stronger than they were when they went in. In 1923, he came to the United States and opened an exercise studio in New York City. Martha Graham (1894-1991), George Balanchine (1904-1983), and Ted Shawn (1891-1972) became his first strong supporters. We owe the current popularity of the Pilates technique to two movements: Many celebrities now use this method of exercise, and trademark restrictions have been lifted, allowing the Pilates name to be used by different training schools.

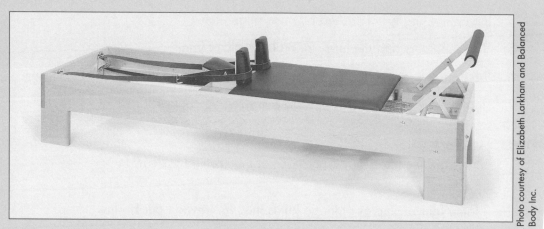

Photo courtesy of Elizabeth Larkham and Balanced Body Inc.

▶ The Reformer is a Pilates exercise machine.

Did You Know? Dance Injuries and Body Conditioning

Structure, strength, and stretch are three aspects that contribute to one's longevity as a dancer. Imperfections in these areas can cause physical injuries over time. Protection from injury may just mean that a dancer must pay attention to and correct these imperfections when training. For example, a person with hyperextended knees (when the knees push back beyond proper alignment of the bones of the upper and lower leg) may have to "reeducate the joint 'memory'" (www.dance-teacher.com/backissues/dec00/dancehealthy.shtml). Structural problems may require the assistance of an expert. Contact institutions such as the Harkness Center for Dance Injuries to find where you can go for help.

We can work on increasing our strength and flexibility to compensate for physical limitations. Find out as much as you can on these two aspects and seek professional help if necessary. One way of working on these areas is through the Pilates method, a method of body conditioning that creates a balance of strength, flexibility, and endurance. You can locate a certified Pilates trainer in your area by conducting a Web search.

After completing your personal movement analysis (lesson 1.4 Take the Stage), use Web sites to gather information on your problem areas.

CHAPTER 1

Review

Name _____ Class _____ Date _____

True/False

1. Muscles can only push. _____

2. The shoulder is a pivot joint. _____

3. Joints are the places where two bones attach. _____

4. Overmuscling is not caused by poor alignment. _____

5. The shoulders and the hips are ball-and-glove joints. _____

6. Less energy is required for movement when the body is aligned correctly. _____

7. To flex your elbow, the triceps do a concentric contraction. _____

Short Answers

1. What are the three major functions of the skeletal system?

2. Name four examples of hinge joints that we have in our bodies.

3. Our wrists and ankles have two different types of joints that allow them to move in different ways. Name these types of joints.

4. Explain or illustrate two different images that describe proper vertical alignment.

5. What is the relationship between a prime mover and an antagonist?

Matching

1. (a) bones   ___ attach muscles to bones
2. (b) joints   ___ support and protect the body
3. (c) muscles   ___ hold the bones together
4. (d) ligaments   ___ pull on the bones to make movement
5. (e) tendons   ___ allow the bones to move

Essay

What would you say to a fellow dancer who wishes that he had been born with the "perfect" dancer's body? How could you help him change his perception of his instrument?

Warming Up and Cooling Down: Personal Rituals

2

▶▶▶▶▶▶▶▶▶▶▶▶▶▶▶▶▶▶▶▶▶▶▶▶▶

▶▶▶▶▶▶▶▶▶▶▶▶▶▶▶▶

▶▶▶▶▶▶▶▶▶▶▶▶▶▶▶▶

From chapter 2 you will

1. be able to explain what constitutes a proper warm-up and know how to create your own personal warm-up;

2. know what constitutes a dance class, understanding the proper etiquette of taking a dance class; and

3. be able to design your own cool-down and stretching ritual.

Overture

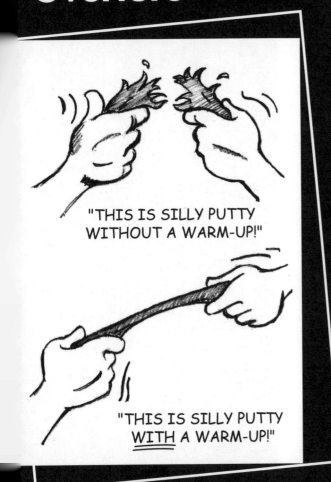

"THIS IS SILLY PUTTY WITHOUT A WARM-UP!"

"THIS IS SILLY PUTTY <u>WITH</u> A WARM-UP!"

Have you ever played with Silly Putty? If you have, you know that when it is cold and you try to manipulate the substance, it tends to snap. Once you have warmed the putty in your hands you can begin to mold it, shape it, and stretch it; it will yield to your wishes. The same is true with your muscles. They need to be warmed before you really begin to use them. Certain muscle groups need to be warmed no matter what you ask them to do. Other muscle groups have to be warmed for specific tasks.

Think of a muscle as a piece of raw, cold, sinewy chicken. It is a stiff substance that is not very pliable. But warm it and it becomes like gelatin in a plastic bag. It is soft and jiggly and can be molded. This need for a warm-up is true for all performers including athletes, musicians, singers, actors, and dancers.

A dance class consists of three parts: the warm-up, the body of the class (which includes learning new skills and perfecting those already learned), and the cool-down.

LESSON 2.1

Your Personal Warm-Up Ritual

5,6,7,8 Move It!

Learning how to control and use your breathing is important to being a good dancer. Practice your breathing technique by breathing in (inhaling) when you prepare for your movements (preparation) and breathing out (exhaling) at the start of the dance sequence.

Vocabulary

hoofer • Bartenieff Fundamentals • movement patterns

Curtain Up

Warming up the body is an essential tool in getting the maximum benefit from any physical activity. By creating the structure of a warm-up, you become much more involved in your conditioning and can tailor the warm-up to your own needs. (See lesson 1.4 in chapter 1, which will help you in creating a warm-up for your specific needs.) You should modify your warm-up as your physical needs change. What movements make your body feel loose and limber? You want a warm-up that is safe.

In addition to your specific needs, you should know what constitutes a complete warm-up. Before beginning a warm-up, think about these ground rules: Make no sharp movements of the neck, always make the knees face the same direction as the toes, and use gentle movements.

The following foundation-building components should be included, in the order listed (McGreevy-Nichols et al. in press):

1. Lubricate each joint, exploring full range of motion and using gentle movements. The lubrication portion of the warm-up

includes an inventory of the joints and muscles and an exploration of how they can be moved. Starting with the top of the body, move your

- head and neck;
- shoulders;
- arms, elbows, and wrists;
- torso;
- hips and legs; and
- knees, ankles, and feet.

This exploration can also be done from bottom to top.

2. Use aerobic movements. Repetitive movements bring blood flow to large muscle groups. Only when there is adequate blood flow to the muscles can you begin to move more fully or quickly. The aerobic portion of a warm-up should include alternating

- jogging in place,
- hopping,
- jumping, and
- skipping.

3. Lengthen large muscle groups. The lengthening portion of a warm-up can begin by exploring how you can

- make your body taller,
- make your arms reach the ceiling,
- make your arms reach the side walls, and
- make your hands touch your toes and then try to straighten your knees.

4. Use crunches and curl-downs for strength.

► Warm-up mode from different dance forms: *(a)* Male ballet dancer at the barre, balancing; *(b)* female modern dancer doing a roll-down; *(c)* Indian dancer doing hand and leg movements.

 # Take the Stage

Knowing your weak and stiff areas will help you determine the best warm-up for you.

1. Create your own personal warm-up. Look to the parts of your body that need to be warmed before you even begin to take a class. Pay special attention to places that may be sore or stiff, and include exercises that will help you perform a particular dance style.

2. Make a concrete plan, listing your specific needs and what movements you will do to accomplish your goals.

3. Once you are secure in the movements that will accomplish your goal of preparing your body, make a short dance using all of your personal warm-up movements.

4. Take note of how your body reacts to the movements in your warm-up. Ask yourself whether your work is improving as a result of your personalized warm-up.

Take a Bow

Look at how your warm-up dance reflects the goals you set for yourself. In your journal answer the following questions:

1. Does the dance have the proper component of a warm-up?

2. Does the warm-up reflect my personal needs as outlined in this lesson's Take the Stage?

3. What do I have to do as a next step in building an extended personal warm-up?

Spotlight: Sammy Davis Jr.

Legendary performer Sammy Davis Jr. (1925-1990) started performing at the age of four with his father and his uncle as part of the Will Maston Trio. They had a vaudeville act and later appeared on the "Ed Sullivan Show" and other variety shows. Sammy continued to perform as a solo act when the two older men retired. He sang and acted as well as danced. Sammy Davis needed hip and knee replacements while still in his performing years. He said that he wished he had known how important warming up was even to a "hoofer" (tap dancer). All those jumps into knee drops while muscles were cold were a large part of the reason that he needed replacement surgery.

Did You Know? Irmgard Bartenieff

Irmgard Bartenieff (1900-1981) was a student of Rudolf Laban (1879-1958), the creator of a system of notating movement as well as the developer of a language useful in observing and describing movement. Building on Laban's work, Ms. Bartenieff created a series of exercises called Bartenieff Fundamentals. These dynamic exercises are meant to improve movement patterns (habitual ways of moving) and connections between body parts and the space around the body. Fundamentals include work with breath, core–distal (center of the body to the ends of the limbs) connectivity, head–tail (head to tailbone) connectivity, upper–lower (upper body to lower body) connectivity, body–half (whole right side to whole left side) connectivity, and cross–lateral (right side crossing oppositionally to left side or contralateral relationships) connectivity. Experience with this work increases a dancer's efficiency of body movement and improves expressiveness. Bartenieff said, "Body movement is not a symbol for expression, it is the expression" (Hackney 2002, p. ix).

For more information, here are some resources:

- Laban/Bartenieff Institute of Movement Studies, 234 5th Avenue, Room 203 (27th Street), New York, NY 10001
  212-477-4299

- Bartenieff, Irmgard with Lewis, Dori. 1980. *Body movement: Coping with the environment.* New York: Gordon and Breach Science Publishers.

- Hackney, Peggy. 2002. *Making connections: Total body integration through Bartenieff Fundamentals.* New York: Routledge.

► *Lesson 2.2*

Dancer's Ritual: The Class

5,6,7,8 Move It!

To begin to understand the importance, for a dancer, of "taking class," do the following activity:

1. Create a dance combination in a form (ballet, modern, jazz, or other) in which you are most comfortable and knowledgeable.
2. Teach this dance combination to another student.
3. After watching your peer dance, give her helpful comments that will improve her performance of this combination.
4. Learn another student's combination and make improvements based on his comments.
5. Discuss with your partner or class how this activity improved dance skills and understanding.

Vocabulary

kinesphere • mark • overtraining • RICE

Curtain Up

Taking a dance class, especially with a new teacher or in a new environment, can be a daunting experience. There are times when so many people are in the class that you are overwhelmed (but then again, what a good place to hide). There are times when only a few people are in the class and you are the new student (a good opportunity to get attention). When you are training to be a dancer, you need to take a minimum of three dance classes per week. This helps you to learn and perfect new skills and maintain peak physical condition.

Following are some hints for gaining the most from taking a dance class:

1. Approach the class with courage and a smile, even though you may be quaking

► Dance class is a way of life for a dancer.

© George Tarbay

in your "boots." Show your interest and be ready to learn something new.

2. Introduce yourself to the teacher, if the opportunity presents itself. But don't take too much time in doing that.

3. If the class is crowded, survey the group. Place yourself between people who look like they know what they are doing—the people who look like they are exuding confidence. You can follow them if you can't see the teacher or if the instruction is unclear. Make your own space (kinesphere—your personal space) and try not to invade the space of others.

4. Work really hard. Don't show despair or get overly frustrated. A new teacher might just let you work on your own for the first class or two before offering corrections and comments.

5. When offered a correction, thank the teacher and apply that correction to your work. Don't argue with the teacher or say that you have always done it differently in other places.

6. Use the mirror as a tool to help you make the given corrections. Don't just gaze into the mirror like a zombie. You should dance with awareness and a sense of performing throughout the class.

7. Show enthusiasm for what you are doing. If you think the class is too easy for you, don't show it. There is no such thing as too simple a class. This scenario gives you time to perfect your technique.

8. Be sure you know the combination before taking a place in front of the room or in front of the line going across the floor. If you find that you do not know the combination, or cannot do the work, step aside quickly to let others have their turn; mark the combination in the corner of the room. Marking means to move through movement without using the full space or energy. Marking is useful both for figuring out combinations and for practicing and memorizing movement. Once you know the combination, you can then take your place in the back of the line and try again.

9. There are rituals for the end of a class. In ballet the instructor may lead the class in a reverence combination. In other dance forms the teacher may have you form a group and do a formal thank-you through movement. In most classes, applauding the teacher and the musician is a traditional way of saying thank you.

 Take the Stage

Reflecting is an essential part of learning. It is important for you not just to go to dance class and then walk out as if nothing took place. You should think about what you did, what your frustrations and achievements were, and what comments your teacher made.

1. Take your classes as usual. For a period specified by your dance teacher, write a journal entry for each class. Be sure to write about the following:

   • The main things that I learned in this class were . . .

   • The most helpful comment that the teacher made was . . .

   • I am going to use this information to improve my dancing by . . .

   • In this class, I noticed that I have improved in the following ways:

2. Using what you learned in a previous dance class, set a goal for a specific improvement that you will concentrate on for your next class. An example might be to land every jump in a proper plié with your heels in contact with the floor and your knees over your toes. Add a fifth item to your journal on taking class by writing your goal for the specific improvement and noting when you have improved on this goal (for example, I want to improve on . . . I noticed that I have made progress toward this goal when I . . .).

Take a Bow

1. With a partner or your class, discuss the importance of taking dance classes on a regular basis. Use the process of journaling and goal setting in this lesson's Take the Stage to document your improvement and use this information to support your comments.

2. Write a journal entry or an essay on the importance of the dancer's ritual of taking dance classes.

Spotlight: The Children of Theatre Street

The Children of Theatre Street is a documentary that highlights the development of young ballet dancers as they pursue their dreams of becoming members of the Kirov Ballet. The video, narrated by Grace Kelly, provides an interesting perspective of what it takes to become a world-class dancer. This video is available through major online bookstores and Princeton Books.

Did You Know? Overtraining

Reprinted from www.sportsmedicine.about.com/cs/injury prevention/a/aa04600.htm.

Contrary to popular belief, pushing yourself too hard can hurt you. When you overtrain you don't allow your muscles to recuperate adequately, and you can actually break down your muscle tissue rather than develop it. The following is some advice from Elizabeth Quinn, available online at http://sportsmedicine.about.com/library/weekly/aa040600.htm?terms=overtraining.

Overtraining occurs when athletes try too hard to improve performance and train beyond the body's ability to recover. The common warning signs of overtraining include the following:

- Mild leg soreness, general achiness
- Pain in muscles and joints
- Washed-out feeling, tiredness, drained feeling, lack of energy
- Sudden drop in ability to run "normal" distance or times
- Insomnia
- Headaches
- Inability to relax, twitchiness, fidgety motions
- Insatiable thirst, dehydration
- Lowered resistance to common illnesses, colds, sore throats

What do I do if I have some of these warning signs?

If you are suffering from several of these warning signs, see your physician so that any potentially serious problem can be ruled out. Otherwise, just stop and rest, and take a few days off. Drink plenty of fluids, and check and alter your diet if necessary. Maybe you can plan an alternate workout routine so that you are not constantly working the same muscle groups. If you don't receive consistent massage work, this would be a good time to get one or two sessions to help flush metabolic wastes out of your system and help loosen up your muscles. To prevent further over-training injuries, check out some of the more common overuse factors. You may need to modify all or part of what you're doing. If you suffer an injury during a workout, just remember RICE (rest, ice, compression, elevation); this could save you a lot of pain, discomfort, and a long recuperative layoff.

Stretch What You Strengthen: Cool Down

5,6,7,8 Move It!

1. After taking a full dance class in your school, share your favorite stretch with the members of the class. Be sure to demonstrate carefully and have your teacher watch for correct alignment and performance of the stretch. Be sure to tell the class which muscles and area of the body that the stretch is targeting.

2. Learn stretches that your classmates share.

3. Pay special attention to stretches that target the areas of your body that are tight (as you noted in lesson 1.4).

 ## Vocabulary

static stretching • passive stretching

 ## Curtain Up

How do you usually feel the day after you have worked especially hard in a dance class or a performance? Do you feel stiff and sore? If you feel bad the next day, you most likely neglected to stretch after your strenuous activity. Your body is trying to tell you that you did not cool down properly. You should develop a ritual (habit) of slow breathing and movements along with stretches. After strenuous activity the muscles and cardiovascular system need to return to normal gradually. You should continue a slow activity until your breathing and heart rate are normal. You need a calming conclusion to the physical activity before returning to your academic activities. During this time of conclusion, you can reflect on the lesson of the day and on what you have learned.

During normal muscle use, the body's circulatory system is able to flush out waste products that are left over after the muscle cells produce energy for movement. When the body is called on to produce greater effort, the circulatory system is unable to immediately remove all waste products. The body responds with soreness and stiffness until the muscle tissue can be cleansed. Stretching tightened muscles allows for better circulation, which helps in the removal of the waste products from the muscle tissue. Slow, gentle movement during a cooldown will also help in improving circulation

► Stretching tightened muscles allows for better circulation.

in the muscle groups used in the dance class or performance.

Stiff muscles affect the full range of motion necessary for efficient, free movement. Poor biomechanics, fatigue, and overuse injuries can occur when the mover does not have full range of motion in a part of the body. Repetitive movement causes muscles to shorten or tighten. Muscles that are short and tense are more prone to tearing and injury. Remember how muscles correspond to their opposites (antagonists). When one side is overly tight the other is stretched, again setting up the dancer for injury. Microscopic tears and repairs (scarring) can also occur with overused or poorly balanced muscle groups. When one muscle group is stronger and used more than another, related group, an imbalance of efficient biomechanics develops. This imbalance can eventually cause injuries. To correct a muscular imbalance, stretch the tight side, and strengthen the weaker muscles. There are various types of stretching. Passive stretching, PNF (proprioceptive neuromuscular facilitation) stretching, CR (contract–relax) stretching, and CRAC (contract–relax, antagonist–contract) stretching are done with a partner and should only be done under careful supervision (McAtee 1993). Here are descriptions of various stretches:

- Static stretching: Slowly lengthen the muscle to be stretched by staying in a fairly comfortable position for 15 to 30 seconds. When the feeling of stretching subsides, you can move into a deeper stretch position.
- Passive stretching: A partner takes the muscle through the stretched range while you (the person being stretched) remain passive. Be careful in this process because the person stretching your muscle can't feel when the muscle has reached the overstretched point.
- PNF stretching: An isometric contraction (shortening contraction with no joint movement and the muscle length remains the same) is done before the stretch. For example, the hamstrings could be stretched in three ways.
  - In the first way, hold–relax, you (the person being stretched) first take the leg into its stretched position, then resist the helper who tries to move the leg into a deeper stretch. You then relax, and the helper moves the leg into a deeper stretch.
  - In the second way, CR, the helper initially resists as you attempt to isometrically move in the opposite way to the stretch. Then you relax, and the helper moves your leg into a deeper stretch.
- The third way, CRAC, is similar, but it is the person being stretched that moves the leg into a deeper stretch after the isometric contraction.

Here are some hints for more effective stretching:

- Stretch what you strengthen. After a workout, pay attention to the muscles that seem fatigued or tight. These are the muscles you should stretch.
- Use your breathing to aid in the stretching process. Exhale and relax into the stretch.
- Do not bounce in a stretch. Bouncing actually shortens the muscle.
- Finally, you should feel stretches not in the joints but rather in the belly (center) of the muscle. If you feel a stretch in a joint, try bending the joint a little or place a rolled towel under the joint for support.
- Most important, do not stretch when the muscles are cold. Stretching sessions should be reserved for after a class or performance.

Practice the following general safety tips at every level during all warm-ups, classes, and cool-downs and other dance and movement activities:

1. When doing knee bends (pliés), keep the knees over the toes.
2. When doing any kind of jump, start from bent knees (plié) and land with bent knees (in plié).
3. Align the spine properly in every exercise. Avoid a hyperextended back or a forward-thrust pelvis.

4. Always make sure there is adequate blood flow to the muscles before stretching (generally after a full warm-up).

5. Make sure shoulders are relaxed and pulled down. Avoid hunching (shortening the neck).

6. If, during any movement throughout the lesson, you feel pain, stop immediately.

7. Take time to cool down by continuing to walk. (Heart rates return to normal at different times. Take whatever time you need to cool down adequately and to be aware and in charge of your own body.)

 Take the Stage

You know best what part of your body needs to stretch because you know what you worked on strengthening. Create a cool-down that you can use after taking a dance class. Base it on the movements you worked on during a class in a specific dance form. Remember the rule *stretch what you strengthen*. Take your personal physical traits into consideration when creating this cool-down. (Relate this to your knowledge of yourself from lesson 1.4.)

 Take a Bow

Write out your cool-down and stretching ritual. Include the reasons you have used certain exercises and stretches. For example, after a class with many jumps, you may want to do roll-downs (forward port de corps) to relax your shortened and compressed back muscles. You may want to stretch your calf muscles after a class that included many relevés.

 Spotlight: Brenda Little

National Ballet of Canada dancer Brenda Little, of Montgomery, Alabama, understands the need for proper warm-up, stretch, and cool-down. She recommends that you keep your feet warm along with the rest of your body. Always listen to your body by paying attention to signs of stress, like sore joints and tired muscles. Always plan a warm-up that suits your body. Avoid aggressive stretching before your body is ready. Staying healthy is more important than how far you can extend your leg (Cornell 2001, p. 106).

 Did You Know? The New York City Ballet Workout

The New York City Ballet has created an exercise regimen that combines stretching and strengthening, helping participants to improve flexibility, cardiorespiratory endurance, and posture. The developers of this workout took into account the additional forms of training that dancers use so that they could provide an equally challenging workout for all audiences. *The New York City Ballet Workout* is available in video, DVD, and book format, which are available online through most large bookstores.

CHAPTER 2

Review

Name _____ Class _____ Date _____

True/False

1. To attain the best stretch you should bounce in the stretched position. _____
2. Your kinesphere is your personal space around you. _____
3. Repetitive movements cause blood to flow to large muscle groups. _____
4. Stretching tightened muscles does not allow for better circulation. _____
5. If I feel pain during any part of a lesson, I should work through it. _____
6. There is such a thing as too simple a class. _____
7. Applauding the teacher is a traditional way of saying thank you. _____

Short Answers

1. What are the three parts of a dance class?

2. What are Bartenieff Fundamentals?

3. What does RICE stand for?

4. When would I use the RICE theory?

5. What are some of the signs of body stress?

6. Where should a stretch be felt?

7. What is a hoofer?

(continued)

Word Find: Some Signs of Overtraining

mild soreness

lack of energy

insomnia

pain in muscles

headache, dehydration

tiredness

colds

```
Z  T  M  A  C  T  B  Y  K  T  O  V  E  H  G  I  M  P
P  A  I  N  I  N  M  U  S  C  L  E  S  S  O  S  T  Z
S  G  L  I  N  E  S  A  C  T  A  U  V  P  S  S  E  T
D  B  D  V  Q  M  L  H  L  A  C  L  A  G  E  S  S  A
I  N  S  O  M  N  I  A  I  T  K  E  I  T  A  P  E  S
S  T  O  R  K  H  J  S  T  U  O  Z  A  O  O  K  U  G
E  I  R  E  N  O  T  S  E  E  F  T  O  H  A  T  S  E
L  H  E  A  D  A  C  H  E  B  E  K  T  S  C  A  L  L
I  N  N  E  R  C  O  V  A  L  N  E  T  I  O  U  T  A
O  K  E  J  H  G  L  A  B  Z  E  K  Y  B  Y  K  L  E
N  C  S  A  T  Z  D  O  T  I  R  E  D  N  E  S  S  Y
U  K  S  O  A  S  S  C  E  D  G  B  Y  K  Y  T  O  K
K  T  D  I  H  D  O  D  E  H  Y  D  R  A  T  I  O  N
```

From *Experiencing Dance: From Student to Dance Artist* by H. Scheff, M. Sprague, and S. McGreevy-Nichols, 2005, Champaign, IL: Human Kinetics.

Choosing a Dance Form That Suits You: Identity Search

3

▶▶▶▶▶▶▶▶▶▶▶▶▶▶▶▶▶▶▶▶▶

▶▶▶▶▶▶▶▶▶▶▶▶▶▶▶▶

From chapter 3 you will

1. decide how you like to move;
2. make realistic observations about your physical traits and abilities; and
3. make choices about your individualized training and preferred dance form.

►Overture

Like to feel connected to the earth

+

low center of gravity

DANCES SUCH AS AFRICAN OR NATIVE AMERICAN

Think of your future in dance as a mathematical equation. The "solution" to the equation may not be your favorite, but it will be logical, and it will offer you the best options and opportunities. Once you see the logic, you can be happy with *your* decision.

►LESSON 3.1

What Are Your Movement Preferences?

5,6,7,8 **Move It!**

Freely improvise (move without planning) movement. Have a partner observe and describe what kind of movements you used most often.

 Vocabulary

improvise • nature versus nurture • ballon

 Curtain Up

How many of your movement behaviors are inherited, and how many are learned? Some of the ways you move are due to your inherited skeletal structure. Environment and experiences also affect the way you move. Also consider climate. People from colder climates tend to move more quickly than people from hot climates do. Steamy, tropical climates tend to encourage slower movement. Movement patterns are built over time. The way you react to your surroundings and imitate how you see other people (like your parents) move build these movement patterns. The movement patterns may eventually become movement preferences. Although your job, as a dancer, is to increase your range of motion and expressive abilities, you will always have a personal preference for particular movements. Following are some possible ways movement preferences could influence the dance style or form that you may most enjoy:

- If you have a good "stretch," then, while improvising, you might notice that you prefer using your leg extensions over using torso movements.

- If you like percussive movements, perhaps you should try tap, flamenco, or Irish step dancing.
- If you are good at doing many isolations at the same time, then Middle Eastern dance and some jazz styles might be appropriate for you.
- If you prefer using a still, erect body or torso, then ballet, Cambodian, and many Western European historical court dances could be ideal for you.

- If you enjoy using the torso, and don't mind being upside down, then modern dance, aerial dance, and break dancing may be a good fit for you.
- If you enjoy studying traditions and codified movements that have a long historical background, try ballet, classical Indian, Balinese, Western court dances, and Native American tribal dances.

© 2003. Steward Photography

© George Tarbay

▶ Different strokes for different folks!

Take the Stage

One of the best ways to begin to create dances is to explore different movements done in different ways:

1. With a partner or the class, brainstorm movements that fall under each of the following descriptive categories: powerful, delicate, sudden, timeless, focused, unfocused or multifocused, controlled, and uncontrolled. For example, some movements that can be considered powerful are hit, slap, kick, punch, press, smash, slash, pound, and haul.

2. Spend time improvising or exploring each of the words under each category.

3. Place a √ next to each of the movements that you like to do the best or are most comfortable doing. Look for any patterns in your preferences.

4. Write a short description of how you prefer to move. Use what you learned in this activity and in this lesson's Move It! to help you analyze your movement preferences.

Take a Bow

When you choreograph a piece for yourself (when you will be the primary dancer) you will probably want to use the movements you like best and you look best doing.

1. Create a dance based on all your preferences. You may use the movements that you improvised in this lesson in addition to other movements. If possible, have this dance videotaped.

2. Create a dance based on the movements in this lesson that you did not choose as your preferences. You may add other related movements. If possible, have this dance videotaped.

3. Write a short essay or journal entry that not only compares and contrasts these two dances but also describes the ways you like to move best (that is, your movement preferences). If any of your discoveries were surprising to you, write about this new information as well.

Spotlight: Rudolf Laban

Rudolf Laban (1879-1958) was a dancer, choreographer, dance advocate, and dance and movement theorist. One of the founders of European modern dance, he collaborated with great dancers such as Mary Wigman (1886-1973) and Kurt Jooss (1901-1979). Laban's biggest contributions to the field, however, were his development of choreology (the discipline of dance analysis) and the creation of a system of dance notation, now known as Labanotation or Kinetography Laban.

Labanotation was used for more than just notating or recording choreography.

In 1942, Laban was asked to investigate the possibility of applying movement notation to industrial processes. The recording of industrial rhythms had, until then, been accomplished by filming the process, but this was no longer possible because of the shortage of film. The need to find some method by which women could be trained to do jobs previously done by men made it imperative to find another way of recording movement. (Thornton 1971)

In an attempt to perpetuate his work, it was thought to form an organization through which his work might become more widely known and to provide a center for all those using Laban's principles of movement. In 1954 the 'Laban Art of Movement Centre' was founded as an educational trust and it was during this year that 'Principles of Dance and Movement Notation' was published. (Thornton 1971)

Did You Know? Georgian Dancers

A culture sometimes dictates how its people move. In Georgian traditional dancing, it is the male dancers who compete with bold movement that requires strength, agility, and incredible elevation (ballon). In contrast, women's movements are reserved, with small and light steps. Key words for doing an Internet search on this topic are "Georgian dance," "Russian folk dance," and "character dance."

► Flying through the air shows strength and power.

Your Physical Traits and Abilities: They May Make a Difference

5,6,7,8 Move It!

Make a list of 8 to 10 dance steps or movements that you are especially good at. Create a dance phrase that emphasizes these abilities. Share this dance phrase with your classmates.

Vocabulary

plastic

Curtain Up

As lesson 2.2 Spotlight explored, the documentary *The Children of Theatre Street* shows the physical examination of young Russian children in an effort to identify their suitability for ballet training. Today many young dancers find it helpful to have body (bone) structure screenings and muscle testing done by physical therapists and dance medicine practitioners. These screenings are used to identify both structural limitations and capabilities. Many dancers use this information about their physical traits to plan their training regimen, and some dancers even use this information to help them choose which dance form and style will provide them the most opportunities.

- Pointe work is easier for dancers who have arches in their feet that are neither too high nor too low. Feet have to be both supple and strong to be optimal for pointe work.

Having the great or big toe and the first toe the same length is also optimal for pointe work.

- The length of a dancer's legs is important in some dance forms. Longer legs are more important in ballet and dancing that requires kick lines. What would the Radio City Rockettes be without their long legs?

- Although flexible spines are sought after in many dance forms, other dance forms call for an erect torso, as in Irish step dancing and Georgian dance.

- The amount of external rotation (turnout), as defined by the hip joint structure, is important in classical ballet, modern dance, and many Western European historical court dances. (Aristocratic court dancers in the 17th century used a leg brace, designed to increase turnout, during sleeping hours.)

- The length of tendons and ligaments determines both flexibility and strength in a dancer's body. If your joints are hypermobile, it's advisable for you to work on strengthening the surrounding muscle groups. If your joints are unusually tight, then a limited amount of lengthening is possible (through stretching in the muscles, never through stretching the tendons and ligaments around the joints). The amount of flexibility and strength is valued differently in various dance forms and styles.

It is an unfortunate fact that a few company directors seek dancers with particular body types. To some company directors, however,

© Robert Powell

▶ A straight back and a winning smile for Scottish dance.

body type is not as important. Some directors choose dancers who are best suited structurally to perform their repertory. This is similar to typecasting in the musical theater and acting fields. However, keep in mind how plastic, or able to change, the human body is. If a dancer follows the correct training regimen, her body type is not necessarily a limiting factor in her options and opportunities. Many dance companies celebrate and embrace differences in physical traits and abilities.

 Take the Stage

Part of learning about dance is viewing it. This way you learn how different companies and different choreographers use the dancers' bodies.

1. View videotapes of various dance companies and performances.

2. Using the Physical Traits and Abilities Analysis handout from your instructor, analyze how the choreographers and directors used dancers' physical traits and abilities in the performances.

Take a Bow

Discuss with the class what you observed. Decide which choreographer would be most likely to use your particular physical abilities. Then ask yourself, "Do I like the way the company dancers move?"

Spotlight: Alonzo King

Excepted from www.danceadvance.org/03archives/alonzoking2/page08.html.

Alonzo King (1954-) is known in the dance world for selecting dancers with various body types. Here are some quotes from Alonzo King that support his viewpoint:

> When I look at artists I really look at their voices. I look at how large their voice is, how clear their voice is. And to be really honest, I'm not really thinking sex at all.

> For me it's the manipulation of energy in making shapes, and the understanding of the artist's powers. There may be someone who, because of who they are, they're strong and they have a leadership, and that may be a woman. And there may be someone who's soft and is able to surrender in the most natural way, and that may be a man. We'll put them together in a certain way.

> For biographical information, search online under key word "Alonzo King."

Did You Know? Body Shapes

Our culture is obsessed with model-thin physiques and a mentality that focuses on the body. Extreme emphasis on body size and shape has caused many people to take extreme measures to conform to this ultrathin look, which sometimes triggers eating disorders. The people who are at risk have other issues such as control or a negative self-image.

►Lesson 3.3

Connecting Physical Traits and Abilities With Movement Preferences: Choosing Your Specialty

₅,₆,₇8 Move It!

Take a combination from a class and change the movements or steps to showcase your best physical traits, abilities, and movement preferences.

Vocabulary

vernacular

Curtain Up

Today, more than ever, dancers must be skilled in many forms and styles of dance. Modern dance choreographers are setting pieces (choreographing) for ballet companies and choreographing Broadway shows. Cultural and vernacular (popular) styles are making their way into the more classical forms. For example, Savion Glover's style is a mix of hip-hop and tap dance. Glover choreographed *Bring in 'da Noise, Bring in 'da Funk* for Broadway and his portion of *Tap Dance Kid*. The people of Sesame Street learned to tap dance from Mr. Glover. The dance world is truly becoming smaller. But most dancers are happiest when they find like-minded people and a style and form of dance that agree with their movement preferences and body types. It is then when artists are most free to discover their unique "voices." This is similar to having the freedom to choose your own group of classmates to work with on a project for dance class. You just know with whom you work best and whose dancing complements or contrasts with yours.

Take as many workshops and master classes as possible so that you have a better opportunity to discover the form and style of dance in which you would like to specialize. You will then be equipped to analyze the "fit" of that form and style to your movement preferences and body type. Remember to be realistic, but if the drive is there, almost nothing is impossible. For more details, see chapter 12.

► A tap shoe that has been worked hard.

Take the Stage

You can be a keen evaluator of your work. You also can assess the way you move in different dance forms:

1. Compare the videotapes that you made in lesson 3.1 Take a Bow with your analysis of the professional dance company videos (lesson 3.2 Take a Bow). Try to watch yourself with a detached eye so that you can make a logical decision about which dance form you would most like to pursue.

2. Discuss your current decision with classmates, teachers, and family members. (Remember that you can always change your mind at a later date.)

Take a Bow

Write a reflective essay about your decision. Support your reasoning with examples and descriptions. Use information and work from lessons 3.1, 3.2, and 3.3. Include goals for your training and realistic plans for meeting these goals.

Spotlight: Isadora Duncan

Isadora Duncan (1878-1927) has had great influence on 20th-century dance. Isadora, a nonconformist in most aspects of her life, thought that dance was a sacred art. She was inspired by classical Greek arts, folk dances, social dances, nature and natural forces, and the American athletic movement. She used free and natural movements that included skipping, running, jumping, leaping, and tossing.

Isadora's style of dancing made use of the solar plexus and the torso as initiation for movement. In opposition to the corseted female fashion, she performed with free-flowing costumes, bare feet, and loose hair. Isadora is considered one of the founders of the modern dance form.

For a greater understanding of Ms. Duncan, read the following texts:

- Daly, Ann. 1995. *Done into dance: Isadora Duncan in America*. Indianapolis: Indiana University Press.
- Duncan, Isadora. 1927. *My life*. New York/London: Liveright.
- Kurth, Peter. 2001. *Isadora: A sensational life*. London: Little, Brown.

Did You Know? Isadorables

The legacy of Isadora Duncan has been kept alive from the initial group of six students from her school, dubbed "the Isadorables." Isadora's choreography has been passed down from one dancer to another in an unbroken line of generations of Duncan dancers. Organizations such as the Isadora Duncan Foundation for Contemporary Dance help keep the spirit of Isadora alive.

CHAPTER 3

Review

Name _____ Class _____ Date _____

True/False

1. Rudolf Laban was one of the founders of European modern dance. _____

2. You will never have a personal preference for particular movements. _____

3. Body screening plays no part in your choosing your training regimen and which dance form you might pursue. _____

4. The length of tendons and ligaments determines both flexibility and strength in a dancer's body. _____

5. Extreme emphasis on body size and shape has caused many people to take extreme measures to conform to a certain look, which sometimes causes eating disorders. _____

6. Today, dancers shouldn't be skilled in many forms and styles of dance. _____

7. Isadora Duncan thought that dance was a sacred art. _____

Short Answers

1. Why do you move in certain ways?

2. What was one of Laban's biggest contributions to the field of dance?

3. Who are the people most likely to conduct proper body screening?

4. What are male Georgian dancers known for?

5. What is one of the reasons that people develop eating disorders?

6. What was Isadora Duncan's style of costuming?

7. Who carries the legacy of Isadora Duncan's dancers?

Matching

1. pointe work ___   (a) external rotation
2. kick lines ___   (b) feet that are supple and strong
3. Irish step dancing ___   (c) length of dancer's legs
4. classical ballet, court dances ___   (d) flexibility and strength
5. modern dance ___   (e) erect torso

Learning More Than Steps: No Such Thing As a Dumb Dancer

4

▶▶▶▶▶▶▶▶▶▶▶▶▶▶▶▶▶

Lesson 4.1 Skills and Strategies You Learn From Studying Dance

Lesson 4.2 Applying Dance Learning Strategies to Other Life Situations

Lesson 4.3 Careers Beyond Performing

▶▶▶▶▶▶▶▶▶▶▶▶▶▶▶▶▶

From chapter 4 you will

1. become aware of skills that you gain by learning through dance;

2. understand that the way dancers function can help you to succeed in life; and

3. learn about dance-related professions and about life beyond dance.

How do you learn to make choices? What in your education helps you to develop that skill? When your mom encouraged you to pick out the clothes you would wear when you were very young, that started the lifetime ability to make choices. When you were asked if you were hungry, that made you think and make a cognitive decision. When you learn to dance and to choreograph, you learn to make decisions all the time. You also learn that before your decision is final, you can make adjustments that will improve your decision.

Skills and Strategies You Learn From Studying Dance

5,6,7,8 Move It!

Rehearse part or all of a dance you are currently working on. (If possible, have this rehearsal videotaped, and view the tape.) Use the rubric on page 43 to evaluate your readiness to perform. (In this process you use critical thinking, analysis, and habits of mind.)

Vocabulary

habits of mind • Bloom's taxonomy • affect • endorphins • metacognition • mutiple intelligences • learn to learn

Curtain Up

Years ago, my (Marty Sprague) dance teacher told me, "There is no such thing as a dumb dancer." Dance educators have always known that studying dance changes and improves the way people think. Now education and brain research are proving these educators right. Dancers and other artists are incredible problem solvers and creative thinkers. They can often see unique solutions to problems. Businesses often employ artists to teach workshops to help employees develop creative-thinking skills. If you analyze the type of work art requires, you'll see that a higher level of thinking is required.

Benjamin Bloom, an educational psychologist, developed a hierarchy of six levels of complexity of human thinking (Bloom 1956). This model is called Bloom's Taxonomy of the Cognitive Domain. Dancers use all six levels of thinking. Following is a description of each level and dancers' use of each level of thinking.

Bloom's complexity of thinking *(Sousa 2001)*	Dancers use
1. *Knowledge:* rote recall of information	1. *Knowledge:* when they memorize and learn dance steps and dance information
2. *Comprehension:* ability to make sense of information	2. *Comprehension:* when they can explain or discuss new dance steps and dance information
3. *Application:* ability to use learned information in new situations	3. *Application:* when they practice and apply new dance concepts and steps
4. *Analysis:* ability to break information into parts so its organization or structure can be understood	4. *Analysis:* when they can compare and contrast different dance styles or forms and when they break a new dance into phrases to learn the dance in smaller parts
5. *Synthesis:* ability to put parts of learned information together to form new plans, patterns, or structures	5. *Synthesis:* when they compose or create a dance phrase or dance
6. *Evaluation:* ability to judge the value of information based on specific criteria	6. *Evaluation:* when they look at a performance and critique it

Think about the type of work you do as a dancer, and decide which kind of thinking you use. Instantaneous evaluation and revision are inherent in dance. For example, before, during, and after the execution of a pirouette, a dancer has an internal dialogue about the success or failure of that particular turn. Some questions that may flash through the dancer's mind are "How was my timing?"; "Because my second spot was slow, was that the reason I fell off

LESSON 4.1

Move It! Rubric for Self-Evaluation on Readiness to Perform

(+) = You are totally confident that you can perform this dance with absolute accuracy, clarity, preciseness of counts, energy, quality, and with the appropriate emotional projection.

(√) = You think that with concentration and a limited amount of practice you can perform this dance with adequate accuracy, clarity, preciseness of counts, energy, quality, and the appropriate emotional projection.

(–) = You do not think that you are ready to perform this dance yet. You need more practice, and you need more help from the choreographer, director, or fellow dancers.

From *Experiencing Dance: From Student to Dance Artist* by H. Scheff, M. Sprague, and S. McGreevy-Nichols, 2005, Champaign, IL: Human Kinetics.

of my second turn?"; "Was my supporting leg fully extended?"; and "How was my alignment?" The dancer may soon forget this evaluation unless he brings it to consciousness and acts on the corrections that he decides are necessary. This thinking and revision process should be repeated and transferred to the next learning experience.

Howard Gardner, an educational and developmental psychologist, proposed that people are smart in different ways. He researched and created a theory of multiple intelligences, or modes of thinking preferences. Dr. Gardner is careful to explain that no one uses only one kind of intelligence, but rather, people usually use a combination of these ways of thinking or a "profile of intelligences" (*The Disciplined Mind*, Gardner 1999, p. 24). The following are Gardner's seven forms of intelligence (*Intelligence Reframed*, Gardner 1999, pp. 41-43):

1. Verbal-linguistic intelligence is spoken and written language ability.

2. Musical intelligence is the ability to communicate thoughts and feelings through music and rhythm.

3. Logical-mathematical intelligence is problem solving and sequential if–then and cause–effect thinking abilities.

4. Visual-spatial intelligence involves visual and tactile abilities to notice and manipulate objects found in the environment, as in visual art or map reading.

5. Bodily-kinesthetic intelligence involves control (conscious or planned and unconscious or trained) over body movements (both fine and gross motor skills).

6. Intrapersonal intelligence is the ability to understand one's self.

7. Interpersonal intelligence is the ability to work in social structures and understand the moods and motivations of others.

Dr. Gardner has since classified other ways of thinking, or intelligences, that include the abilities to observe and classify (naturalist intelligence) and to think in a spiritual or philosophical way (existential intelligence) (*Intelligence Reframed*, Gardner 1999, pp. 48-52 and 60-64). Educators and brain researchers now use this idea of intelligences to support the theory that people learn in different ways and at various speeds and that they are better at using certain skills over others. How many times have you visualized, sketched designs, written about, felt, or moved an idea for a dance before actually creating the artwork?

Albert Einstein would have been categorized as a kinesthetic thinker because he said that he felt the movement of his theories first, and the numerical formulas came later.

Arthur L. Costa is an emeritus professor of education at California State University at Sacramento and codirector of the Institute for

► Dancing can change your outlook.

Intelligent Behavior in El Dorado Hills, California (Costa and Kallick 2000). With Bena Kallick (an educator and consultant) he worked with the idea that certain thinking skills or behaviors help us function in all types of learning situations. These habits of mind can be taught and transferred to various activities. The following are some habits of mind (Costa and Kallick 2000, p. xii):

- Persisting
- Managing impulsivity
- Listening with understanding and empathy
- Thinking flexibly
- Thinking about thinking (metacognition)
- Striving for accuracy
- Questioning and posing problems
- Applying knowledge to new situations
- Thinking and communicating with clarity and precision
- Gathering data through all the senses
- Creating, imagining, innovating
- Responding with wonderment and awe
- Taking responsible risks
- Finding humor
- Thinking interdependently
- Remaining open to continuous learning

In creating a new piece of choreography, the choreographer and the dancers must apply all these habits of mind to their work.

Dance learning can have a positive impact on your emotions (also known as affect). Exercise and movement release hormones in the brain, called endorphins, which are mood elevators. Have you noticed that if you go into a dance class depressed, you usually leave in a better mood? Participating in a dance project also increases self-esteem, which can increase a person's comfort level in taking risks in a new learning experience. Dance is healing. Dancing about a troublesome event or issue can help both the dancers and the audience heal emotionally. Doing or watching a light-hearted dance can lighten the moods of dancers and audience alike. Think back to dances that have made you either cry or laugh out loud.

 ## Take the Stage

You can learn through observation. But just observing is not enough. You should record what you observe.

1. Observe a dance class or rehearsal.

2. Using the Thinking Skills and Habits of Mind Checklist from your instructor, put a check next to an item every time you see it being used.

 ## Take a Bow

Evaluating and analyzing is another tool for learning.

1. Looking at the list, determine which items received the most checks.

2. Write a short lab report on your findings. Include examples from the class or rehearsal that support your findings.

Spotlight: The Arts Education Partnership

The Arts Education Partnership is a national coalition of arts, education, business, philanthropic, and government organizations that demonstrates and promotes the essential role of the arts in education. This organization has been responsible for many important documents that contain research that supports the role of arts in learning. Two of these documents, *Critical Links: Learning in the Arts and Students' Academic and Social Development* (2002) and *Champions of Change: The Impact of the Arts on Learning* (1999), are of particular value in advancing the role of the arts in education.

Did You Know? The Process Is the Process

Good thinking is basic to all learning. When you learn to learn, you learn to adapt your own learning style to whatever subject you are covering. There are proven ways to learn. Table 4.1 shows and compares the progression of thinking steps in the creative and artistic process to those in the scientific, problem-solving, and writing processes.

► TABLE 4.1 **Comparison of Cognitive Processes**

	Creative and artistic	Scientific	Problem-solving	Writing
1. Concept	Choose topic	Ask question and define problem	Define problem as a question	Identify topic
2. Investigation	Research topic	Research and collect data	Research and investigate	Do general research
3. Exploration	Identify important aspects of topic	Revelation, see a method, generalize	Get many solutions	Collect ideas, expand research
4. Selection	Devise problems to be solved, ask questions	Develop hypothesis	Choose best solution	Limit subjects
5. Development	Solve problems and produce material	Experiment or test, verify or prove false	Check validity of solution	Write first draft, self-evaluate, rewrite
6. Refinement	Design artwork, self-evaluate, revise	Write final peer evaluation	Try out solution	Do first review of final draft
7. Exhibition	Get and use feedback from performance or show	Publish response to feedback: acceptance or criticism	Get feedback and do final evaluation of solution	Publish and receive public response

Applying Dance Learning Strategies to Other Life Situations

5,6,7,8 Move It!

Explore the idea or inspiration of circles by working in three different modes: drawing, creative writing, and dancing. (If your teacher gives you a rubric, make sure you refer to it as you work on your dance composition or study.) Your dance study is an exploration of an idea through the creation of a short dance.

1. Drawing: Draw designs inside three circles. The inspiration or subject matter for the drawing should be circles. The first circle should represent the beginning of your idea or expression; the second circle should represent a middle development of the idea or expression; and the third circle should represent the conclusion of the idea or expression.

   Criteria:

   • Artistic skills and processes are used to express the inspiration or subject matter of circles.

   • The problem of expressing the symbol and idea of circles is solved in this drawing.

2. Creative writing: Write a paragraph based on the inspiration or subject matter of circles.

   Criteria:

   • The topic is about circles.

   • The paragraph is at least six sentences in length.

   • The paragraph has a topic sentence.

   • The paragraph explains or develops your idea in a middle section.

   • The paragraph has a conclusion.

   • In this paragraph you will demonstrate proper grammar, punctuation, spelling, and usage.

3. Dance study: Create a dance study about circles.

   Criteria:

   • Circles appear in floor patterns (pathways that dancers make on the floor as they move through space) and air patterns (pathways that dancers make in the air as they move through space).

   • Circles are made using different body parts (isolations).

   • The dance study is long enough to express the complete idea.

   • The dance study has a clear beginning (shape or entrance), middle (development of the main idea), and end (shape or exit).

   • The dance study includes both locomotor and nonlocomotor (axial) movements.

   • The dance study uses a variety of dynamics.

   • The dancers memorize the dance study and perform it with no breaks in movement.

Vocabulary

transfer • dance study • air patterns • floor patterns • beginning, middle, and end • locomotor movements • nonlocomotor movements

Curtain Up

The creative process is the same no matter what someone is making. Refer to the Comparison of Cognitive Processes table in lesson 4.1 Did You Know? Notice the similarities between the creative and artistic processes and the writing, problem-solving, and scientific processes. You can apply what you know through choreographing, learning dance skills, and performing to any other life or learning situation. Taking new learning from one situation and applying it to another situation is called transfer.

In this lesson's Move It! you were asked to create a drawing, a piece of writing, and a dance phrase. Consider what you learned about your creative process. Was your thinking similar in all three tasks? Did all your pieces clearly communicate the inspiration of circles? Was the structure of beginning, middle, and end helpful to you in each task? Which discipline were you most comfortable using? (This may tell you something about your preferred learning style.) If you paid attention to your thinking (metacognition, or thinking about thinking) while you were working on the task that you were best at, and applied this way of thinking to your least favorite task, then you performed the skill of transfer (applying a learned skill to another task).

- You can use the self-discipline you have learned in technique classes and rehearsals in any training situation. Self-discipline is needed in such diverse activities as playing sports, memorizing facts for a test, and staying on schedule for a project.

- The teamwork skills that you have learned in rehearsals, performing, and group work in choreography will be useful in any committee work you do in the future. Listening to all ideas, giving your input, compromising on decisions, and being responsible for your assigned work are all teamwork skills you have learned in dance.

- Persistence is necessary for completing research or when problem solving. Dancers, detectives, and scientists all have persistence in common.

- Transfer what you know about rehearsing and performing in dance to any other performance or exhibition situation, whether this situation is a theater production or an oral report given in school.

- Being an artist has taught you about risk taking (putting yourself and your ideas out before others). The self-esteem and self-confidence you have gained through successfully completing and performing a dance will serve you well when you are confronted with new experiences.

- Dancers should know how to stop and evaluate their work and abilities. They learn how to take their work apart, decide what is good and poor about it, and make revisions. Evaluation is necessary for all types of work, from writing a term paper to serving on an advisory panel for the government. Without evaluation, improvement is impossible.

- Creative thinking flows easily for experienced dancers. Some artists have described the creative state of mind as almost like being in a trance. Use creative thinking when rearranging information or making anything original.

- Of course, the sense of responsibility and the ability to work hard are traits that all serious dancers share, and you should apply those skills to your employment opportunities.

Dancing teaches more than just steps. Bring all that you have learned from dancing and apply it to the rest of your life. Remember, there is no such thing as a dumb dancer!

▶ You can use critical thinking skills that you learn as a dancer to solve problems in the professional world.

 # Take the Stage

Do this small experiment to observe thinking skills and habits of mind in another activity and in comparison with the thinking skills and habits of mind used in dance.

1. After obtaining permission, attend a planning meeting at a place of business or at your school. Use the Thinking Skills and Habits of Mind Checklist from your instructor to evaluate the thinking skills and habits of mind that you observed being used in the meeting.

2. Compare your list from lesson 4.1 Take the Stage with this list.

3. Write a lab report to document this comparison.

4. Create a dance lecture/demonstration (see lesson 12.2) in which you highlight the thinking skills and habits of mind that are used in a class or rehearsal.

▶ Students giving a lecture/demonstration.

Take a Bow

Present this lecture/demonstration at a faculty meeting, school committee meeting, parent–teacher meeting, or business forum.

Spotlight: Mitchell Korn

Reprinted, by permission, from M. Korn, *The Artvision team: Biographies* (Rineback, NY: Artvision). www.artvision.com/bimk.html.

Mitchell Korn is the founder and president of Artsvision and is widely regarded as North America's leading arts education innovator and practitioner. Mr. Korn is credited with returning arts education to America's great urban centers: New York, Chicago, Detroit, San Francisco, and other cities.

The *Wall Street Journal* called him America's "one-man arts education industry." He was the 1993 recipient of *Parents Magazine* As They Grow Award in the Arts, honoring his efforts in "making the world a safer, healthier, and happier place for children."

Even as the field of arts education faces hard economic times, Mr. Korn and Artsvision continue to be asked by the country's most prestigious institutions to develop and improve their education initiatives. Mr. Korn also continues his work in artist training, teacher training, staff professional development, strategic planning, and fund-raising advice for clients.

Did You Know? Careers in and out of Dance

Your involvement in dance education can prepare you for almost any career path you choose. After reading this chapter, think about and record what skills, processes, and dispositions are attributable to your dance training.

Careers Beyond Performing

5,6,7,8 Move It!

To understand how one career can be related to another and how one career can lead to another, do the following activity:

1. Improvise and set (memorize) a short series of movements.

2. Choose the movement that you like the best.

3. Improvise and set another short series of movements based on this favorite movement.

4. Repeat items 2 and 3.

Vocabulary

freelance consultants

Curtain Up

Many careers and occupations are related to dance performing. Of course, the occupations of choreographer and dance teacher easily come to mind. The production side of dance performances includes stage manager, lighting designer, stage technician, costume designer, seamstress, and house manager. Artistic director, assistants to the artistic director, and choreographer are also related careers.

Many more occupations may prove of interest to dancers. Dance science and dance medicine encompass such occupations as kinesiologist, dance therapist, physical therapist, physical trainer, movement therapist, and nutritionist. Dance education has become a field in itself and can easily mesh with certi-

fied positions in public and private educational institutions at elementary, secondary, and higher education levels. Dancers are hired to help athletes in other sports such as skating, diving, and gymnastics. Gymnastics coaches hire choreographers to work with gymnasts on their floor and beam routines. Figure skaters spend a lot of time with choreographers. Dancers have found themselves moving into the literary field and writing for newspapers and magazines and publishing books on a myriad of dance topics. Arts management positions include general manager, business manager, fund-raising manager, grant writer, and publicity and booking agent. Public service (arts councils) and policy making (task forces,

▶ Physical training is an alternative occupation for people with dance training.

Spotlight: Rhee Gold and Linda H. Hamilton

Adapted from www.americandanceawards.com

Often we think there is only one way to apply our dance learning: through performance. Rhee Gold (1961-) is an example of a person who has expanded his interest and talent in the field of dance to include a variety of accomplishments:

- He has been codirector of the Sherry Gold Dance Studios in Brockton, Massachusetts.

- He was a professional dancer.

- He has been a master teacher serving on major convention faculties, including Dance Masters of America, Dance Educators of America, Dance Olympus, and the Second International Congress of Dance in Brazil.

- With his family he established the American Dance Awards as a fund-raiser for their dance company. Today, it is one of largest and most-respected competitions in the world.

- He was elected to serve as the president of Dance Masters of New England and went on to become the youngest president ever elected of the Dance Masters of America.

- He helped to establish UNITY, an association of dance-related organizations from the private, K-12, and higher education sectors.

- He joined forces with Gloria Jean Cuming to establish Project Motivate, a business and motivational seminar for dance educators and studio owners.

- He is a lecturer and motivational speaker presenting at dance-related organizations across the United States and Canada.

- He has been an educational columnist for *Dance Magazine* and also serves as the "Teacher Talk" columnist on *Dance Magazine's* Web site.

- He created and began publishing the *Goldrush* newsletter in the late 1980s, which is one of the most respected sources of information for more than 15,000 dance educators across the United States and Canada. The newsletter, whose focus is positive dance education, is published four to six times annually.

- He has formed the Rhee Gold Company, which is a multifaceted venue through which dance teachers can explore new philosophies for the classroom and enhance the service, organization, and success of their dance schools (including Project Motivate).

- He is in the process of publishing *The Complete Guide to Teaching Dance: An Insider's Secrets to Personal and Financial Success.*

Linda H. Hamilton went from dancing with the New York City Ballet to earning a doctorate in clinical psychology. She is currently a monthly columnist for *Dance Magazine,* addressing the concerns of young dancers and their parents, and has a private practice in New York City. She has written a book, *Advice for Dancers: Emotional Counsel and Practical Strategies,* that is the result of years of research with more than 1,000 dancers across the country (Hamilton 2002). In it she outlines strategies for dealing with a variety of physical and psychological issues that concern dancers.

association leaderships, and volunteering) often require the dancer's special abilities. The retail business for the dance field is also lucrative for book, music, film, clothing, and equipment companies. Many dancers have become freelance consultants (people who are hired for limited times by groups, institutions, and organizations) and presenters (those who lead informational sessions at workshops and seminars), as well as in-house employees of larger organizations and institutions. As you can probably tell by the list of occupations, ways to use thinking skills and habits of mind that are learned in dance are only limited by one's imagination, which is also enhanced by dancing.

 ## Take the Stage

As you approach the time to make decisions about your life's work, you should make sure that you learn all there is to learn about a chosen occupation.

1. Choose one of the occupations of interest to you that is listed in this lesson's Curtain Up.

2. Research this occupation. Try to find information on job responsibilities, type and amount of training necessary, and places one can go to get this training. If possible, interview someone who is currently working in this occupation.

 ## Take a Bow

After you have completed research, it is a good policy to record the information you've gathered.

1. Develop an oral or written report on this occupation.

2. Present this report to your class. Take notes on the occupations presented by your classmates.

3. Keep this information in your journal for future reference.

 ## Did You Know? People Dancing Longer!

Dancers are performing well later and later in their careers. With advances in dance medicine, kinesiology, and training methods, older dancers are capable of maintaining physical capabilities that allow them to continue performing at a very high level. Another reason for acceptance of older dancers is the large number of baby boomers that are currently dancers and audience members. There is a greater value placed on the contributions that older performers can bring to the art of dance. To learn more about older dancers, do a search for "older dancers" on the Internet.

CHAPTER 4

Review

Name _____ Class _____ Date _____

True/False

1. Dancers are critical thinkers. _____

2. Benjamin Bloom listed 12 levels of thinking. _____

3. Instantaneous evaluation and revision are not inherent in dance. _____

4. People learn in different ways and at different speeds. _____

5. Good thinking is basic to all learning. _____

6. Dancers do not need teamwork skills. _____

7. Dancing teaches more than just steps. _____

Short Answers

1. How does Bloom's application of ability to use learned information in new situations apply to dance?

2. Who researched and created a theory of multiple intelligences?

3. What famous person mentioned in lesson 4.1 would be categorized as a kinesthetic thinker, and why?

4. In what other situations can you use the self-discipline you have learned in technique classes and rehearsals?

5. Why is improvement impossible without evaluation?

6. How can what you know about rehearsing and performing in dance transfer to any other kind of performance or exhibition?

Essay

Write a brief essay about how you learn. Explain how learning to dance has prepared you to learn other things outside of dance.

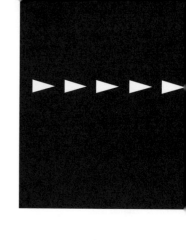

Expressing Ideas and Emotions: One Movement Is Worth a Thousand Words

▶▶▶▶▶▶▶▶▶▶▶▶▶▶▶▶▶▶▶▶▶▶▶

▶▶▶▶▶▶▶▶▶▶▶▶▶▶▶▶

▶▶▶▶▶▶▶▶▶▶▶▶▶▶▶

From chapter 5 you will

1. be able to use dance to express your-self without words;

2. be able to communicate important ideas and concepts without words; and

3. be able to address world and com-munity issues through dance.

►Overture

"She was so happy, she jumped for joy." "He was so rushed, he looked like a dog chasing his tail." How many expressions do you know of where the person's mood or emotion is described by movement? "He was as nimble as a monkey" brings to mind the image of someone able to climb and swing and hang with great ease. Sometimes movement can show far more than words can. When you receive a wonderful gift, what do you do before you say thank you? You rush and hug the gift giver!

►LESSON 5.1

Dance As Nonverbal Communication

5,6,7,8 Move It!

Sit in a place where you can watch people as they walk by. Some suggested sites are shopping malls, parks, school cafeterias or hallways, and hotel lobbies. Study the way different people walk. Later, in the dance studio, create a dance study based on these different types of walks.

 ## Vocabulary

body language

 ## Curtain Up

We are surrounded by words, written and spoken. From the moment we get up in the morning until we go to sleep at night (and even while we sleep), our brains are processing words. But is communicating with words the only way? As dancers, we know that this is not so. Without saying a word, dancers can move audiences to laughter, tears, anger, and contemplation.

In your experience, you know immediately how your friends are feeling before they utter any words. You read their body language. Are they walking slowly with their eyes downcast and their chests sunken? Then they are probably tired or depressed. Are they quickly bouncing down the hallways with twinkling eyes and upright posture? Then they are probably happy or excited. Mabel E. Todd, author of *The Thinking Body: A Study of the Balancing Forces of Dynamic Man* (1937), said, "We judge our fellow man much more by the arrangement and movement of his skeletal parts. . . . Living, the whole body carries its meaning and tells its own story, standing, sitting, walking, awake or asleep" (p. 1). This quote describes the term

► After watching the many movements that can happen in a crowd of busy people, you can create a dance study based on the movements you see.

body language. A dancer's training takes the body's expressive ability and magnifies it. For example, an upraised arm, depending on how it is held, can express anger, yearning, or joy. A performer should be able to communicate the exact meaning of a movement and even take on another person's movement preferences and postures.

According to Dr. Judith Lynne Hanna, PhD, senior research scholar in the department of dance at the University of Maryland at College Park, "Movement is our mother tongue and primordial thought. Infants track movement and anticipate what will come, as in the peek-a-boo game. Recent research underscores the power of nonverbal communication, showing that it is sometimes even more compelling than verbal communication" (Hanna 2003, p. 1). Dance can build a rapport between and among people. Dance is used in courtship in many cultures. War dances are used to synchronize warriors' strength and intentions. Dance therapy can build bridges of communication. Why do many dance companies do a group warm-up before a concert? Moving together with the same energy, rhythm, and purpose bonds people together.

Take the Stage

When you put emotions and feelings into movement, the movement may have a greater effect on you and your audience than words ever could.

1. There is a Native American saying that states that you cannot truly understand another person until you have "walked a mile in his moccasins." Working with a partner with whom you are most comfortable, each of you creates a separate short solo. These solos should be based on an important event in your individual lives or descriptive words about each of your personalities. (You may wish to expand on or include movement from lesson 3.1 Take the Stage, since these are your movement preferences.)

2. Teach each other your solos, and coach each other to performance level.

Take a Bow

Observation, analysis, and recording cement in your mind what you have learned.

1. Share these solos with your class.

2. Discuss with your partner what you learned about each other.

3. Write about the process of walking a mile in another person's moccasins.

Spotlight: Schools for the Deaf That Teach Dance

Can people who cannot speak express themselves through dance? Can they dance as part of a dance company? The answer to these questions is yes, most definitely! Many schools for the hearing impaired have dance as part of their curriculum. The Kwa Thintwa School is a haven for those who are excluded from a general education. This South African school enriches the education of all the children with dance. They use dance as an alternative method of communication. Gallaudet University, the only American university for the deaf and hearing impaired, is in Washington, D.C. They have a dance company and have developed methods for teaching hearing-impaired dancers. You can learn more about dance for the hearing impaired and Gallaudet University by doing a Web search using the following key words: "Gallaudet University+dance," "deafness+dance," "dancers with hearing loss."

Did You Know? The Nonverbal Dictionary of Gestures, Signs & Body Language Cues by David B. Givens

The items in this dictionary have been researched by hosts of specialists in the fields of anthropology, archeology, biology, linguistics, psychiatry, psychology, and semiotics. This publication is from the Center of Nonverbal Studies, headed by David B. Givens, PhD, of Spokane, Washington. Go to an Internet search engine and enter key words such as "nonverbal communication" and "communication without words."

Dance As a Wordless Report or Essay

5,6,7,8 Move It!

Think about a topic that you are studying in another subject area. Pull out any ideas or concepts that can be expressed through movement, and create a short dance study based on these ideas or concepts. (For example, the westward expansion of the United States could be communicated through a progression of movements from stage left to stage right and include movements that represent wagon trains, land rushes, working the land, and herding cattle.)

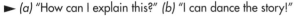
► *(a) "How can I explain this?" (b) "I can dance the story!"*

Vocabulary

nonfiction • narrative

Curtain Up

Dances have to be about something. They can be celebrations of rites of passages, narratives, abstract expressions of ideas, or even explorations of movements themselves. Have you ever considered that a dance can fulfill the requirements of a report or essay? The research you do on the subject can act as inspiration for your dance.

After gathering information through the various research methods, narrow your focus so that you can select the main inspirations for your dance report. You can do this in two ways. You can sort your information into like categories. These categories become a source for dance phrases or sections of a dance. A second way is to select important quotes or excerpts from written sources and then create dance movements to communicate the ideas or images to help bring your topic to life. Once you have movement and dance phrases, you are ready to design your dance report. Refer to chapters 8 and 9 to help you do this.

Through the years many ballets have been created to tell a story of significance or to relate a biography. Some of these ballets are well known and are often performed, whereas others are relegated to live in books about dance. Some examples follow.

- *After Eden,* choreographed by John Butler (1967), is a story about Adam and Eve after they were expelled from the Garden of Eden. The choreography portrays the feelings, good and bad, that Adam and Eve experienced. The audience goes through the emotions of the lovers and finally sees them face together whatever life has in store for them. Although revived by Joffrey City Center Ballet in 1972, it now remains unperformed. This is an example of a dance based on a biblical account, as was *Prodigal Son,* choreographed by George Balanchine (1929).

- *Anastasia,* choreographed by Kenneth MacMillan (1967), tells a story out of history. It involves a Russian princess whose family goes through the Bolshevik Revolution. Anastasia is thought by many to be the sole survivor of her family. The ballet starts with Anastasia as a child and concludes with her in a Berlin hospital recalling her life. There are still unanswered questions, but that just adds to the mystery. This ballet is in two acts, so there is plenty of time to tell this historical story.

- *Billy the Kid,* choreographed by Eugene Loring (1938), tells a story about the opening of the West. It was first presented by Ballet Caravan in Chicago with music by Aaron Copland. Eugene Loring played Billy. This one-act ballet includes both documented facts and fictional lore about the old West. It is a story about a kid who was born in New York and taken to Kansas when he was 3 years old. He killed a man for the first time when he was 13 and was shot dead when he was 21. Also, it is a story about his life, not just the headlines.

- *Cinderella, Sleeping Beauty, Coppélia,* and *The Nutcracker* are examples of full-length story ballets. They depict fairy tales and have been produced and reproduced by dozens of dance companies and choreographed by many early– and modern–day choreographers.

- *Fall River Legend,* choreographed by Agnes de Mille (1948), is about a historic event. It tells the story of an infamous double murder and the town's reaction to it. The full-length ballet is based on the murders of Andrew and Abby Borden by their daughter Lizzie. It was premiered by Ballet Theatre with Alicia Alonzo playing the lead. Nora Kaye was supposed to dance the role but fell ill. She did dance all the subsequent performances and became known for her dramatic quality and presentation.

- *Monument for a Dead Boy,* choreographed by Rudi van Dantzig (1966), is a retrospec-

tive of a teenaged boy who, on his death, looks back on his life. It uses an electronic score. It was first performed in the United States by the Harkness Ballet in 1967. It was revived by American Ballet Theatre in 1973. This ballet was a precursor to the actual use of spoken text within the dance. The text that precedes the ballet is a quote from Truman Capote, "Unafraid, not hesitating, he paused only at the garden's edge where, as though he had forgotten something, he stopped and looked back at the bloomless, descending blue, at the boy he left behind" (Capote 1948, p. 231). There are verbal themes for the eight parts of the ballet, which are taken from *The Inner Wallpaper* by Hans Lodeizen.

- *Romeo and Juliet,* Shakespeare's version of star-crossed lovers, is another wordless account of a timeless tale. It was choreographed and performed many times and by many companies, but first by Leonid Lavrovsky in 1940 to the Prokofiev score. Each company brings different angles to its productions, and each varies in length and intensity. The first version, from Russia, was in 13 scenes with a prologue and an epilogue. There was a film version made in 1954. Antony Tudor choreographed a one-act ballet for Ballet Theatre in 1943. He did not use the Prokofiev score. Tudor's ballet was revived by American Ballet Theatre in 1971. Frederick Ashton, Kenneth MacMillan, and Robert Joffrey were among other choreographers who choreographed and presented this ballet over the years.

You might find it interesting to go to the Internet and look up various choreographers to see how professional choreographers have brought nonfiction and narrative subject matter to the stage. (Nonfiction themes are taken from history, current events, or social issues. Narrative themes tell a story).

Take the Stage

Create a moving biography through a dance study.

1. Select a figure or personality from past or present, and do the research on that person's life.

2. Choose the most important aspects of that person's life.

3. Create a dance study representing these aspects.

Take a Bow

Use the following rubric to complete and evaluate your dance report:

LESSON 5.2

Take a Bow: Rubric for Moving Biography

Above standard: Evidence of research is included (notes, handouts); important aspects of subject's life are identifiable in the dance report; choreographic elements and forms are visible in the dance report (see chapters 8 and 9); choreographers have evaluated and revised their dance reports. (There is evidence in the form of evaluation handouts or notations in their journals and videotapes of this revision work.) Dance report is presented to the class for evaluation.

At standard: Evidence of research is included (notes, handouts); important aspects of subject's life are identifiable in the dance report; choreographic elements and forms are visible in the dance report (see chapters 8 and 9); dance report is presented to the class for evaluation.

Needs more work: Any one of the "at standard" items is missing.

From *Experiencing Dance: From Student to Dance Artist* by H. Scheff, M. Sprague, and S. McGreevy-Nichols, 2005, Champaign, IL: Human Kinetics.

Spotlight: Charles Weidman

Charles Weidman (1901-1975) created many ballets and was known for his more satirical and whimsical comedies. He and Doris Humphrey (1895-1958), his dance partner for more than 20 years, also choreographed for Broadway and New York City Opera as well as for their own company, the Humphrey-Weidman Company. In his younger years he partnered with Martha Graham and danced with Denishawn (Ruth St. Denis and Ted Shawn's dance company) for eight years. He founded a school with Doris Humphrey and, after her death and his decline in the limelight, he started another school that was a smaller version of the one he had with Ms. Humphrey. Some of his students include Sybil Shearer, Jack Cole, José Limón, and Bob Fosse. With these students he formed the Charles Weidman Dance Company. One of the works he created for this company was *Lynchtown* (Brown 1979).

Did You Know? Lynchtown

Lynchtown, from suite *Atavisms*, choreographed by Charles Weidman (1936), is about mob mentality as it tells the story of a hanging of an African American in Omaha in the early 1930s. Mr. Weidman was born in Nebraska in 1901. He felt it was important for him to tell this story. Not once during the piece did he allow the dancers to address (face) the audience. The choreography has them in profile, intent on what they see as their task: the hanging. It has a profound effect on the audience (how removed the audience feels while they are sucked into the story).

Photo courtesy of Julie Strandberg.

► Reconstruction of *Lynchtown* at Brown University.

The Peaceful Route: Dance As Social Commentary

5,6,7,8 Move It!

Watch the evening news or CNN. Almost always there is a social commentary or demonstration by groups of people. Turn the sound off, watch their body language, and make up movement that shows how a crowd would move in protest.

▶ Movement is all around us—just observe!

Vocabulary

poignant • Muganda dance

Curtain Up

You are familiar with the expression "a picture is worth a thousand words." In the case of dance, movement is worth another thousand words. When you create a dance that depicts a particular event from a particular time, you have the ability to leave the audience with a lasting impression, an impression so strong that it will be remembered long after the performance. When you deal with an intense subject through the choreographic process, you will have a greater appreciation and understanding of the event and its place in history.

Pearl Primus, who lived from 1919 to 1994, spoke through her choreography. Not only was she a dancer and choreographer, but she also earned her doctorate in anthropology from New York University. With this educational background she was able to tell the history of the African American in terms of historically and socially significant themes. Many of her pieces showed her deep emotional and intellectual feeling about democracy and the African American striving for liberation and justice. In 1944, as research for some of her more famous protest dances and articles, Pearl Primus took a trip to the Deep South, where she lived and worked alongside African American sharecroppers. Author Lynne Fauley Emery (1988) states,

Primus' "dances of protest" could be considered 'message' dances; compositions designed to draw attention to the inequities and injustices in the lives of American Negroes. "Strange Fruit," for example, dealt with the reaction of a woman toward a lynching. "Hard Time Blues," on the other hand, was a protest against share-cropping. "The Negro Speaks of Rivers," based on the well-known poem by Langston Hughes, was a protest against general ignorance of the black heritage in America. (p. 263)

The slogan of the Workers Dance League was "Dance is a weapon in the revolutionary class struggle." The Workers Dance League was an organization that sponsored concerts, contests, and theater and dance publications. It was connected to the union and communist movements of the 1930s. Cultural activities were important parts of the demonstrations and rallies of these times. The people's movements affected both the subject matter for dances and the collaborative dance-making methods of the 1930s. Some of the famous choreographers and dancers that were involved in the Workers Dance League were Anna Sokolow and Sophie Maslow.

The authors (Helene Scheff, Marty Sprague, and Susan McGreevy-Nichols) remember viewing a concert where the choreographers were schoolchildren. The most memorable piece was done by a 13-year-old boy who had no real dance background. This piece was about the Holocaust. It was simple, elegant, and poignant (moving and touching), and it showed a sense of history and protest. The audience was in tears. No words about the horrific event could have made a bigger impression.

 ## Take the Stage

Dancing about an event brings that event to life. By doing the work of creating, you will learn much more about your topic than you would have had you done only a written report.

1. Choose a subject either from history or from a current event that deals with a protest. Research it. Discuss it with your group and begin to create movement that depicts the subject and how the protestors would move in that setting.

2. Create a dance study that communicates the event or idea. Be sure that the dance study includes movement that expresses the personal significance that the event has for you.

 ## Take a Bow

The following tasks will help you do a short survey of how effective dance studies can be.

1. Write a report on the same topic as you researched for the Take the Stage activity.

2. Present the report in two different ways to two different audiences. To one audience, present just the report (you have the option of either reading your report out loud or presenting the information in oral report form); to the other audience, present both the dance study and the report.

3. Have the audiences evaluate the effectiveness of both presentations.

Spotlight: Dance of Zambia

Muganda dance from Zambia is an example of dance as a means of social commentary. People of Tumbuka have a high rate of illiteracy and very little access to mass media and ways of expressing themselves on current issues. The Muganda dance allows them to express their views and feelings. For example, the lyrics and dance steps might protest a legally polygamous man who shows favoritism to his younger wife while ignoring his first wife. Often young people from different villages meet, interact, and admire each other. It is not uncommon for young men and women who meet at a Muganda dance to marry.

Did You Know? Dances of Protest

Dances of protest happen in many countries and in many times. Following are four very different examples of dances of protest.

1. On the Turtle Mountain Reservation, people protest outside the tribal housing authority office on a daily basis carrying signs that read "Mold Kills Infants" or "Evacuate." Children do traditional dances in protest of the contamination in housing on the Turtle Mountain Reservation.

    Adapted from www.mnpa.org/poy/2001/package/first/a.html.

2. The *Seann Triubhas* dance originated as a political protest dating back to 1745 when wearing a kilt was an act of treason. Pronounced "shawn trews," this Gaelic phrase means "old trousers." The graceful steps reflect the restrictions imposed by the foreign trousers. The lively, quick time in the dance re-creates the Highlanders' celebration of rediscovered freedom.

    Reprinted, by permission, from Hope's Highland Dancers, The highland dances (Anaheim, CA: The Hirschl School of Dance Arts). www.highlanddancer.com/thedances.htm.

3. *Snow Falls*, created in 1967 and set to music by the same name, is a famous Korean dance of protest. It is one of four dances that are labeled a masterpiece in the repertoire of the Democratic People's Republic of Korea. The theme of the dance is enhanced with set decor and props, including a red flag. *Snow Falls* features a female soloist, who carries the flag high, and a corps of female dancers. The soloist represents a guerilla fighter from the People's Republic of Korea; she's braving the cold and snowstorm. The other dancers symbolize the snowfall; they express their deepest feelings about the revolutionary struggle against the Japanese.

    (www.kcna.co.jp/item/2002/200202/news02/27.htm)

CHAPTER 5

Review

Name _____ Class _____ Date _____

True/False

1. Words are the only way to communicate. _____

2. Body language is your body's way of expressing your feelings. _____

3. The first person to choreograph the ballet *Romeo and Juliet* was George Balanchine. _____

4. Agnes de Mille choreographed a piece about a double murder. _____

5. Two famous choreographers and dancers that were involved in the Workers Dance League were Anna Sokolow and Sophie Maslow. _____

6. South Korean women of the Korean people's revolutionary army danced and sang a union song in an anti-government rally. _____

Short Answers

1. Who, according to the information in lesson 5.3, spoke through her choreography, and about what did she speak?

2. Why do many dance companies do a group warm-up before a concert?

3. How does Mabel E. Todd describe the term *body language?*

4. Dances can be about many topics. List some.

5. Name two of the ballets that are based on tales from the Bible.

6. Name one of four dances of protest as described in lesson 5.3.

7. What was the Workers Dance League?

Essay

Write a short essay describing a current event and how you would depict this event in a dance.

Changing Movement to Dance: Dance As an Art Form

▶▶▶▶▶▶▶▶▶▶▶▶▶▶▶▶▶

▶▶▶▶▶▶▶▶▶▶▶▶▶▶▶▶▶

From chapter 6 you will

1. learn to distinguish everyday movement from dance;
2. understand how dance can be a theatrical form; and
3. develop your own aesthetic sense (your likes and dislikes).

►Overture

"The best art entertains." —Garth Fagan

Art should be shared. If you do your art in a closet, with whom will you share it? Art can also educate. If you want audiences to come back for more, they need to be pleased by the performance. Aesthetics, which is a science in and of itself, cannot tell you what is pleasing. Each of us has our own aesthetic—likes and dislikes. A show or a dance company survives and thrives not always by what the critics think and say but by what the audiences see and like.

►LESSON 6.1

Movement Is Everywhere: When Is It Dance?

5,6,7,8 Move It!

Pretend that you are drinking a glass of water. Do the literal (real-life) movements of picking up a glass, lifting it to your lips, tipping it up, and setting it back down. Create a dance study from this idea by making the movement more abstract. "Abstract movement expresses a quality or characteristic apart from the real subject matter" (McGreevy-Nichols et al. 2001, pp. 19-20). Change the literal movements by changing the rhythm, the speed, or the size; repeat movements; put movements into different body parts; add contrasting or opposite movement reversals of order; mix in other, unrelated movement; interrupt or take a detour from the original action; and finally, let the movement grow and change.

Vocabulary

literal movement • abstract movement • battement

Curtain Up

All dance is movement, but not all movement is dance. From the moment of conception until death, the human being is in motion. Movement means life. The difference between movement and dance movement is found in the intention of the mover. There is a certain awareness that dancers bring to movement. This awareness makes the movement more important. A dancer's awareness, intention, and attention bring movement to a more symbolic or universal state. Eric Franklin (1996a, p. 4) states, "Intention is the beginning of every movement. Focusing on a body part with the intention of moving it in a certain direction creates energy that supports movement in this direction. If you focus on a movement a split second before you initiate movement, the ensuing movement will be clearer."

Dance movement can be abstract and symbolic but still convey emotion and meaning. Consider a simple battement (kick). Depending on how the movement is done (which dynamic is used), this kick can represent a break for freedom, an attack, a high-spirited gesture, or even a lazy swing. If choreographic elements, such as levels, size, direction, facings, and rhythms, are added, then the battement's meaning grows in importance. The following are other examples that show how everyday movement becomes dance:

1. A plain walk becomes dance when you change the levels and directions, add arm movements, and alter pace and rhythm.

2. The process of standing up from and sitting down in a chair becomes dance when you conjure up different ways of doing it and add torso, head, and arm movements.

3. Jumping for a basket or swinging a tennis racket becomes dance when you follow through the end of the move or make a move leading up to the jump or swing.

► A dance can move from one level to another.

 Take the Stage

When does everyday movement become dance? When you make it so! Use the following steps to prove the point.

1. As you did in this lesson's Move It!, choose a simple, everyday activity.

2. Do the movements of this activity as slowly, importantly, and directly as possible. Your intent should be to transform this activity into a ritual.

3. Use the suggestions in this lesson's Move It! and include some ideas from the Dance Ideas List Handout on page 73 to create an abstract dance phrase based on this everyday activity.

4. Organize the ritual and the abstract dance phrase into either an AB-structured or ABA-structured dance. (You can decide which element, the ritual or the abstract dance phrase, is the A section and which element is the B section.) See chapter 8, lesson 8.3, for an explanation of AB and ABA.

© 2003. Steward Photography

► You can dance about anything! Your imagination can change movement into dance.

Take a Bow

Comparisons are an effective way of assessing work. By going through the following steps, you will come to a consensus about the two versions of your dance phrase.

1. Perform this dance for your class (and for a videotaping) in two different ways. In the first way, go through the motions, or perform the dance with minimal attention and intent (just enough to execute the steps). In the second way, perform the dance with clear intent and awareness (giving each movement full attention).

2. Ask your classmates to write down and then share with you their observations about both performances.

3. Look at the videotape of your performances, and complete a task evaluation of this activity.

Spotlight: The Grand Union

The Grand Union, a collaborative performance group (1970-1976), explored the link between improvisation and performance; the relationships among choreographer, performer, and audience; and the connection between movement and language. They, along with other groups in the late 1960s and early '70s, challenged the established norms in theater and dance. To accomplish this they combined ordinary, everyday movements with dance. For more information on Grand Union and its members refer to the following books:

- Banes, Sally. 1994. *Writing dancing in the age of postmodernism.* Hanover, NH: University Press of New England.
- Bremser, Martha, Ed. 1999. *Fifty contemporary choreographers.* New York: Routledge.
- Brown, Jean Morrison, Ed. 1979. *The vision of modern dance.* Princeton, NJ: Princeton Books.

Taking the Stage: Dance Ideas List Handout

Instructions: Choose the dance skills and qualities that best express the idea, theme, or image of your chosen dance phrase. For more information, refer to chapter 8.

Movement Skills

[ ] balance   [ ] fall and recovery   [ ] isolation   [ ] weight shift

Locomotor Movements

[ ] walk   [ ] hop   [ ] jump   [ ] leap   [ ] assemblé (jump from one foot to two feet)
[ ] sissonne (jump from two feet to one foot)   [ ] slide   [ ] skip   [ ] gallop

Nonlocomotor Movements

[ ] bend   [ ] twist   [ ] stretch

Movement Qualities

[ ] smooth   [ ] swing   [ ] percussive   [ ] collapse   [ ] vibratory

Movement Elements (Laban's Efforts) *[see chapter 11, lesson 11.1]*

Weight:	[ ] strength	[ ] lightness
Time:	[ ] sudden	[ ] sustained
Space:	[ ] direct	[ ] indirect
Flow:	[ ] bound	[ ] free

Effort Elements (Laban Effort Actions) *[see chapter 11, lesson 11.1]*

[ ] dab   [ ] punch   [ ] float   [ ] glide   [ ] wring   [ ] press   [ ] flick   [ ] slash

Choreographic Elements

Organizing Dancers in the Dance

[ ] facings of dancer

Manipulating Movement

[ ] repetition   [ ] variety   [ ] abstract movements   [ ] literal movements   [ ] levels
[ ] size of movements   [ ] changes in tempo   [ ] floor patterns   [ ] air patterns

Guiding Audience's Attention

[ ] focal point   [ ] stillness

Did You Know? Aerial Dance

Adapted from www.projectbandaloop.org/mission.html.

Aerial dance has been around since the 1970s. Are the performers dancers? Gymnasts? Aerialists? Circus performers? According to Amelia Rudolph, founder and artistic director of Project Bandaloop, Aerial dance is a movement generated by the cross-pollination of dance, climbing, and aerial work. The dance sense of it comes in with the artistry, the connection of one movement to the next. To find more on this exciting new dance form, go to an Internet search engine and type in the words "aerial dance."

© Coreyography L.L.C.

► Have you ever thought of this as dance?

Dance As a Theatrical Form

5,6,7,8 **Move It!**

Choreograph a simple combination of steps. Keep the combination short and basic. Do the combination for peers or a partner. Vary the dance phrase to make it more theatrical or flashy. Share it again. Discuss the differences.

Vocabulary

concert dance • Broadway ballet •   theatrical dance • trade show • *Butoh*

▶ Balinese dance is an integral part of both the culture and religion of the Balinese people.

Curtain Up

When dances are created with the audience in mind, they become theatrical dances. A constant consideration of both the dance makers and the performers of the dance is the audience's reaction. In cultural and social dance forms the dancers' attention is on each other. In improvisational situations the main focus is the movement exploration itself.

Dance as a theatrical form can be traced through the ages. The Greeks and Romans used dance in their theater epics. We can trace dance as part of many forms of theater throughout history. Most of us think of theatrical dance as it has been performed recently. We think of Vaudeville, operas, musicals, films, and nightclub extravaganzas, but we should also think of the more formal dance concerts and dance company performances known as concert dance. Most recently dance has become commonplace in TV commercials, music videos, and at trade shows. (Trade shows are actually minishows that advertise a product.)

Some theatrical dance reflects the culture of the time in which it was created. Some reflect the time and place of the production. All are influenced by mixtures of native and imported dance forms. Some are completely traditional, and some are variations on traditions. Choreographers meet with artistic and production teams to establish which dance forms should be used in any particular production.

Some of the dance forms that are represented on Broadway and in film are traditional ballet, modern, jazz, tap, ethnic and folk, cultural, African, social or ballroom, and historical. Broadway musicals sometimes have dance sections that promote the flavor of the production but do not necessarily have anything to do with the show. "Song of a Summer Night" from *The Most Happy Fella* is one such example of Broadway ballet. These are pieces that set a mood but don't necessarily move the story forward. Sometimes, dance takes over the show, as it does in *The Lion King* and *A Chorus Line*.

Take the Stage

Some of the best choreography starts with an improvisation.

1. Find some time to be alone and improvise either freely or on a topic. Write a reflection on where your attention was focused during this experience.

2. With a small group, either work on a social or cultural dance form or do a group improvisation. Discuss, then write a reflection on where the group's attention was focused during this experience.

3. Either alone or with a group, perform a work designed to be presented to an audience. Write a reflection on where your attention was focused during this experience.

 Take a Bow

Again, using the tools of comparing and analyzing brings you insights into your experiences. Try the following:

1. Discuss the differences among the three types of dance experiences. What were the similarities and differences? Consider the purposes, energies, internal versus external attention of the dancers, and how all these factors affected the dancing.

2. Using your personal dance experiences and any observations of solo improvisation, social or cultural dance forms, and theatrical forms, write an essay that compares and contrasts these types of dance experiences.

▶ Eastern dance has many forms including (a) Cambodian and (b) Indian.

Spotlight: Takaya Eguchi, Soko Miya, and Sankai Juku

The United States is not the only country to have theatrical dance as part of its dance culture. Japan has at least 40 dancers and companies that represent *Butoh*, a postmodern movement. Takaya Eguchi and Soko Miya founded a modern dance school in Tokyo after studying with Mary Wigman in Germany, hence the likeness to postwar German modern dance. It has similar intensive use of imagery. Sankai Juku, a dancer in the *Butoh* movement, was included in the 1984 Los Angeles Olympic Arts Festival. Recently, Western dance audiences and performers really began appreciating Eastern dance culture and their version of postmodern dance.

Did You Know? Kabuki Theater

Kabuki theater was founded in the 17th century by a woman, Okuni, who brought her unique dance style to Kyoto, at the time the capital of Japan. Over the next 300-plus years it matured into a highly stylized theater form in which men play women's roles. Dance is very much a part of what happens on stage. Kabuki theater and dance pieces may be about historical events or everyday life, with the audience coming away understanding the whole story line. Kabuki is dependent on makeup, costuming, sets, and music to help the performers tell the story.

Your Aesthetic Statement: Dance It!

5,6,7,8 **Move It!**

Construct a dance phrase that includes only movement that you consider pleasing or beautiful. Compare your dance phrase with a classmate's phrase.

Vocabulary

aesthetic

Curtain Up

Two definitions of *aesthetic* are "pertaining to a sense of the beautiful" and "a philosophical theory or idea of what is aesthetically valid at a given time." No two people or two time periods have the same opinion of what is good and beautiful. John Travolta's execution of disco dancing in the movie *Saturday Night Fever,* all the rage in the late 1970s, now looks silly and dated to many of the hip-hop generation. As you may have discovered, you and a classmate may have totally different ideas on what types of dance and art are valuable and beautiful. A single person may change her aesthetic sense over time. As a person grows, learns, and has different experiences, her aesthetic sense goes through a type of evolution.

Your aesthetic sense, along with your training, personal movement preferences, and physical structure, could be said to form your personal style, or as they say in literature, your voice. What you dance about and how you dance are influenced by what you consider beautiful and valuable.

 ## Take the Stage

When you choreograph, you are the designer of the movement. You make the choices of what looks and feels right. The Dance Ideas List is a tool that helps you make these choices and decisions.

1. Using the Dance Ideas List on page 73 in lesson 6.1, choose only the movements and choreographic elements that you like best. Add these to your dance phrase from this lesson's Move It! Also, refer to chapter 8 for further explanation.

2. Add your movement preferences from lesson 3.1 Take a Bow. Combine these three dance studies to make a solo that represents your aesthetic sense and voice.

 ## Take a Bow

Observation and reflection, then analyzing and recording document the creative process.

1. Share your solo Take the Stage with your classmates, and watch their solos.

2. After you watch one another's solos, take a few moments to write down the ways in which you saw one another move. Share these reflections with one another.

3. From the sharing of the reflections of your classmates, write an essay describing your personal style and voice.

 ## Spotlight: Larry Lavender

Larry Lavender (1954-) has written and taught dance criticism to many people across the states. In his book, *Dancers Talking Dance* (1996), he gives dance students an introduction to and explanation of his five-step ORDER to critical evaluation of your choreography experience. They are observation, reflection, discussion, evaluation, and recommendations for revisions. Mr. Lavender says, "Drawing on approaches to critical evaluation already in place in aesthetics and in the philosophy of art, the ORDER approach to critical evaluation is based on the idea that to respond critically to a dance, or any work of art, is to discuss it. . ." (Lavender 1996, p. 3).

Did You Know? Changing Dance Preferences Midcareer

Dancers have been known to train in one dance form and then perform in that form. More recently, we have seen many prominent performers and choreographers cross over to other dance forms, sometimes at the height of their careers. Following are three examples.

Mikhail Baryshnikov (1948-), along with Mark Morris (1956-), founded the White Oak Dance Project. Baryshnikov, a successful dancer in the former Soviet Union, came to the United States and worked his magic with many ballet companies and dancers. The White Oak Dance Project is dedicated to exploring the boundaries of modern dance.

Twyla Tharp (1941-) studied many kinds of dance as a young woman, but after she got a degree in art history she joined the Paul Taylor Dance Company. She left to start her own company that focused on avant-garde movement. She has shown her great musical insight by choreographing for films, Broadway, major ballet companies, and television.

Photo courtesy of Pat Berrett.

Photo courtesy of John Brandon.

► During training or a career, a performer such as Bill Evans may change dance form preferences.

CHAPTER 6

Review

Name _____ Class _____ Date _____

True/False

1. All dance is movement, but not all movement is dance. _____

2. Aerial dance is a form of dance in which the performers do flips without using their hands. _____

3. When dances are created with the audience in mind, they become theatrical dances. _____

4. The Greeks and Romans did not use dance in their theater epics. _____

5. A single person can never change her aesthetic sense over time. _____

6. What you dance about and how you dance are influenced by what you consider beautiful and valuable. _____

7. Twyla Tharp got a degree in art history. _____

Short Answers

1. What are some of the choreographic elements that can make a movement's meaning grow in importance?

2. When does a plain walk become dance?

3. What was the Grand Union?

4. What are some of the dance forms that appear in Broadway productions?

5. What are two definitions of *aesthetic*?

6. Larry Lavender gives dance students an introduction to and explanation of his five-step ORDER to critical evaluation of the choreography experience. What are the steps?

7. Who founded White Oak Dance Project?

Matching

1. ballet ___   (a) Takaya Eguchi, Soko Miya, and Sankai Juku
2. *Butoh* ___   (b) May O'Donnell
3. modern dance ___   (c) Larry Lavender
4. dance criticism ___ (d) Robert Joffrey

Connecting to Community and Tradition: Dance As a Cultural, Historical, and Social Form

7

▶▶▶▶▶▶▶▶▶▶▶▶▶▶▶▶▶▶▶▶▶▶▶▶▶▶

▶▶▶▶▶▶▶▶▶▶▶▶▶▶▶▶▶

From chapter 7 you will

1. learn the part that dance plays in different cultures;

2. gain a better understanding of periods in history through dance; and

3. learn how the social mores of the times affect popular dance.

Whether you live in New England, the Southwest portion of the United States, Australia, New Zealand, Greece, Poland, or South America, you have a cultural past. It may not be directly visible, but with a bit of research you can find a history of the reasons your ancestors danced. Dance is part of all cultures, and humans have always danced. What fun it is to find what motivated your ancestors to dance and to pass this information and practice to others!

Cultural Dance

5,6,7,8 **Move It!**

Close your eyes. Imagine a traditional dance pose or step from a culture other than your own. Open your eyes and *do it!* Ask a classmate to identify the country by your demonstration of the step.

Vocabulary

world dance

Curtain Up

Dance is for everyone, but it means different things to different cultures. In many cultures dance is not separated from everyday life. It is used in religious rites and ceremonies, and for many it can be a rite of passage, a thanking of the gods, or the raising and quieting of spirits. Dance is also a way to celebrate, with the movements, meanings, and techniques being handed down from one generation to the next. Men dance with men, women dance with women, and men and women dance together.

You can delve into your cultural background and find movement and material that can be used in building dances. Look to your heritage. In the United States everyone or their ancestors, except Native Americans, have come from another country. Whatever your ancestral background might be, there should be someone around who remembers some of the reasons people of your culture danced. If you do not have firsthand or secondhand knowledge, you can rely on traditional research methods. You can pull information from videos, pictures, artwork, the Internet, and other written sources.

World dance is a term currently used to describe dances that stem from within an ethnic culture and express the movement aesthetic of that culture. It is a global term and has evolved from the term *ethnic dance*. World

► Folklórico dance is one example of world dance.

dance includes the folk dances in which widespread participation identifies it as part of the way of life of the country. World dance is not to be confused with the classical theatrical forms of ballet, modern, and jazz.

Tribal dance can also be under the umbrella of the term *world dance*. It stems from a time before industrialization and is inherent in community life. It is not used for entertainment and is usually serious in nature, done at times of rites of passage, before battles, at victory celebrations, and as mourning rituals. Sometimes it is even used as a way to communicate with the supernatural.

 Take the Stage

This activity has you create a dance based on the research of a particular country or region. It would be helpful for you to have access to videos of ethnic, folk, or world dances; music from various countries; and reference books on various countries. Before you begin, look at the criteria, make sure the original dance depicts the country, fits the music, and is accurately re-created from the video or research. The facts gleaned from the research should appear as part of the dance and should be documented.

Finally, the dance should have a clear beginning, middle, and end. You could look to your local or state arts organization for help in finding a cultural group that specializes in dance from your chosen country.

1. Choose a country or area of a country.
2. Research it.
3. Create an original dance or re-create a dance inspired from observing dances from that specific country.

Take a Bow

When you want to assess your work, you need something to function as a guide. Each criterion is attainable. Part of your job is to identify the answers to the following questions.

LESSON 7.1

Take a Bow: Criteria and Rubric

Criteria for a Cultural Dance

Does the original dance depict the country?

Does the dance fit the music?

Was the dance accurately re-created from the video?

Is there evidence of research?

Do facts gleaned from the research appear as part of the dance?

Has the dance-making process been documented?

Does the dance have a clear beginning, middle, and end?

Rubric

(+):   The dance addresses all criteria and is executed at performance-quality level. Piece is revised based on evaluations from a teacher, a peer, and self. Completed portfolio work.

(√):   The dance addresses all criteria and is shared with the class. Completed portfolio work.

(–):   The dance is missing some of the criteria. Portfolio work is not complete or revised.

Score _____   Evaluator _____   Peer _____   Self _____

From *Experiencing Dance: From Student to Dance Artist* by H. Scheff, M. Sprague, and S. McGreevy-Nichols, 2005, Champaign, IL: Human Kinetics.

Spotlight: Ballet Folklórico de México de Amalia Hernández

Ballet Folklórico de México de Amalia Hernández is a troupe that started with only eight dancers. They performed the traditional folk dances of Mexico. Along came Amalia Hernández's vision that her dancers should be trained in classical ballet and modern so that she, as master choreographer, could introduce the elements of those dance genres into the folk dance traditions. This was one of her greatest innovations. As a touring group Ballet Folklórico de México has brought to the world the richness and mystery of Mexican culture.

Did You Know? Arts and Cultural Organizations That Include Dance

Most state councils on the arts have someone on staff that is responsible for keeping a list of cultural organizations that include dance in the communities. This person might also have information about classes, performances, traditional costumes, and internship possibilities. You may be able to find the phone number for your state council on the arts in the government listings in your phone book or on your city or state's home page on the Internet. Often, cities have their own council on the arts. They are sometimes referred to as alliances.

Historical Dance

5,6,7,8 Move It!

Choose a historical dance form. Improvise movement that you think might be related to a historic period.

Vocabulary

madrigal dance • muse • Terpsichore • tapestry

Curtain Up

Dance occurred even in ancient times. History and social studies classes can study how the dances of past and current societies reflect trends and popular cultures of the times. Dance as a performing art is comparatively recent. The Greeks in ancient times performed their dances in amphitheaters. In medieval times, madrigal dancers entertained in the streets. Madrigal dancing was fashionable during the 16th century and later. It was popular in Italy, France, and England. Ballet developed in Europe and was bandied about, and finally one of its main centers was based in France; hence the vocabulary of ballet is predominantly French.

Historical dance could have been the social, theatrical, or cultural dance form of its day. Now we look back on what has been handed down; documented in traditional and non-traditional forms; and reinvented from cave drawings, tapestries, and drawings of court activities.

- Cave drawings give us the sense that dance was an essential part of everyday life. There were dances for plantings and harvests, for rites of passage, and for needed weather changes.

- Ancient civilizations such as Egypt left dancing to the lower order of people.

They also had professional dancers that could be considered the theatrical dancers of the time. Much of their dancing was documented by the works of sculptors and pottery designers. The Greeks made dance part of their lives, bringing it into their religious ceremonies. They even had Terpsichore as a muse of dance (a muse is a mythical goddess). Romans thought dance was not suited to their dignitaries. They left it to the lower classes. Dancing by priests was a part of public worship. The Romans also had a funeral dance, as did the Spaniards later on.

- Spanish dance can be documented back to the Hellenic period. The art of dance and the number of people dancing grew when dance was incorporated into the church.

- The peoples of Asia cultivated dance. The Japanese and the Indians set aside girls to become their professional dancers. The styles are very different from each other and from the ball dances of Europe. Japan has religious dances in which the fan plays an important part, possibly even suggesting a fan language.

- Native Americans integrated dance and drumming into the very fabric of their lives. For them it was social entertainment, a way to celebrate, a way to welcome the seasons, and a way to ward off spirits.

- Tapestries give us a view of dance from a different perspective. An artist would sketch out a scene of a dance and then an expert needle craftsman would replicate it on canvas. Tapestries were prominent in the renaissance and romantic eras, and there are many tapestries from Eastern cultures as well.

- Court dances were for the enlightened, upper-class people. They were very formal, regardless of the country of origin. Some historians say that the folk dances of the time worked their way into the courts, where they were formalized and codified by the "dance master" of the particular court. A look at Brueghel's paintings of

► Gold coins adorn Egyptian dance costumes.

► In this Mexican dance, the hat is the center of the dance activity.

► Most Native American dances are religious in nature and not for public viewing. The ones that are leave the crowds wanting to see more.

► Court dancers assume specific positions

people dancing in village squares will give you an insight on how the dance masters could create court dances from folk dances.

 ## Take the Stage

Before you start to create a historic dance, look at the criteria you need to satisfy. Does the original dance depict the time period? Find music authentic to the time period. Make sure the dance fits the music. Use artwork, books, or videos in your research. Make sure the dance includes what you learned, and document it. The dance should have a clear beginning, middle, and end.

1. Choose a time period from the list that appears in the Curtain Up section.

2. Through traditional or new methods (Internet, videos), research the dances done.

3. Take some of the positions or steps you have learned through your research, and make a short dance study.

4. Research music that fits the time period.

5. You can work in groups, or you can do your own creating and then teach it to classmates.

Take a Bow

When you want to assess your work, you need something to function as a guide. Each criterion is attainable. Part of your job is to identify the answers to the following questions.

LESSON 7.2

Take a Bow: Criteria and Rubric

Criteria for a Historical Dance

Does the original dance depict the time period?

Does the dance fit the music?

Was the dance accurately re-created from a video or artwork?

Is there evidence of research?

Do facts gleaned from the research appear as part of the dance?

Has the dance-making process been documented?

Does the dance have a clear beginning, middle, and end?

Rubric

(+): The dance addresses all criteria and is executed at performance-quality level. Piece is revised based on evaluations from a teacher, a peer, and self. Completed portfolio work.

(√): The dance addresses all criteria and is shared with the class. Completed portfolio work.

(–): The dance is missing some of the criteria. Portfolio work is not complete or revised.

Score _____   Evaluator _____   Peer _____   Self _____

From *Experiencing Dance: From Student to Dance Artist* by H. Scheff, M. Sprague, and S. McGreevy-Nichols, 2005, Champaign, IL: Human Kinetics.

Spotlight: Selma Jeanne Cohen

Selma Jeanne Cohen (1920-), dance critic, historian, and lecturer, has edited hundreds of books on dance, dancers, choreographers, dance criticism, and dance history. Her most encompassing work is the six-volume *International Encyclopedia of Dance: A Project of Dance Perspectives*. She has appeared as guest lecturer at many universities and was one of the starting faculty members at the High School of Performing Arts in New York City. She was equally comfortable in the worlds of ballet, modern, and Broadway. Ms. Cohen has interviewed famous people in the dance field, has written about them, and is extensively published. As a dance historian she queried whether all dance could be looked at by the same standards or aesthetics.

Did You Know? An American Ballroom Companion: Dance Instruction Manuals

The Library of Congress has a collection titled *An American Ballroom Companion: Dance Instruction Manuals*. The more than 200 social dance manuals start with a late 15th-century source and end with a 1929 publication "Public Dance Halls, Their Regulation and Place in the Recreation of Adolescents." This collection is an online presentation that includes historic materials as well as dance instruction manuals.

Social or Vernacular Dance

5,6,7,8 Move It!

Put on some current dance music.   Improvise to it!

Vocabulary

footsteps • Lindy hop

Curtain Up

Dance has always been a social activity. Part of courting, dance as a social activity is a reflection of social mores and customs often dictated by the music of the day. Such vernacular dance, or popular dance done to vernacular music, is bound by what popular culture will accept. The young are the experimenters with new dance forms, often to the chagrin of the establishment. The minuet of the French courts and the waltz of Austria were social dances that were not initially accepted at the time. The black bottom dance of the Roaring Twenties was thought shocking but is now part of history. Likewise, the watusi from the 1960s is now only nostalgia for those who danced their sneakers off during that period. Disco dancing was the rage of the '70s. Of course, all this time the Virginia reel, square and line dancing, and folk dancing from the melting pot of cultures were popular and are being kept alive in schools, social halls, recreational dance societies, and grange halls.

The Lindy hop, also known as the jitterbug, reappeared on the social dance scene as swing dance. The Lindy was popular in the '20s, but was not as popular during the '30s. During World War II, it became popular again and was known as the jitterbug on the East Coast of the United States and as swing on the West Coast. Because it is joyful, wild, and wonderful, people of all ages are currently learning and dancing this form. The tango, popular in the '20s, has also enjoyed a resurgence. The Argentinean tango became popular because it includes an improvisational element. Cities around the globe have night clubs devoted to the art and fun of Argentinean tango. The

▶ Two examples of social dance include *(a)* salsa and *(b)* tango.

mambo underwent changes and is now done as the triple mambo or cha-cha.

Social dance forms that were established by 1935 are often called traditional social dance. It was not taught but rather handed down through example, friends, and family. It was not until Arthur Murray and other schools of social and ballroom dance were established that the responsibilities of passing on the dances were left to teachers. Examples of traditional social dancing forms or event types include:

- alpine,
- Argentinean tango,
- balboa,
- cajun,
- ceili (traditional Irish dancing),
- Charleston,
- circle mixers,
- contra,
- Irish set,
- Lindy hop,
- mambo,
- old-time waltz,
- polka,
- ragtime,
- Scandinavian,
- Scottish (country or folk),
- square,
- vintage,
- Zwiefache, and
- zydeco.

© Bruce Davis

► Ballroom or traditional social dance is still enjoyed today.

 Take the Stage

Create a dance based on a social dance form. Before you start to create your dance, look at the criteria. Your dance should depict a current social dance and fit the music you have chosen. Make sure you document the dance-making process. The dance should have a clear beginning, middle, and end.

1. Think about the social dances you do today.

2. Using one of the dances, isolate a few of the movements.

3. Take those movements and create a short dance study that is more theatrical than social.

4. Use a popular piece of music.

5. Teach the dance study to classmates.

 Take a Bow

When you want to assess your work you need something to act as a guide. Each criterion is attainable. Part of your job is to identify the answers to the following questions.

LESSON 7.3

Take a Bow: Criteria and Rubric

Criteria for a Social or Vernacular Dance

Does your dance depict the current dance?

Does the dance fit the music?

Has the dance-making process been documented?

Does the dance have a clear beginning, middle, and end?

Rubric

(+): The dance addresses all criteria and is executed at performance-quality level. Piece is revised based on evaluations from a teacher, a peer, and self. Completed portfolio work.

(√): The dance addresses all criteria and is shared with the class. Completed portfolio work.

(–): The dance is missing some of the criteria. Portfolio work is not complete or revised.

Score _____ Evaluator _____ Peer _____ Self _____

From *Experiencing Dance: From Student to Dance Artist* by H. Scheff, M. Sprague, and S. McGreevy-Nichols, 2005, Champaign, IL: Human Kinetics.

Spotlight: Arthur Murray

Arthur Murray (1895-1991) was not born dancing, but he started teaching ballroom dancing in 1912 during the evenings. After a few years, he became known as a leading dance teacher to the members of the upper class. This is was the start of what was to become the national chain of Arthur Murray Franchised Dance Studios. He created and designed instruction books using outlined foot patterns that he called footsteps. He established a place for people to come together to learn and socialize. His ad campaigns became known worldwide with a slogan he coined, "How I Became Popular Overnight." In the early 1920s, others saw how Mr. Murray's studio system could be very profitable and filled with fun; thus the franchise of the Arthur Murray Studios began. The art of social dancing became established and flourished at the hands of Arthur and Kathryn (his wife) Murray and their successors. Arthur and Kathryn had their own national television show for several years, showing Americans that "putting a little dancing in their lives" was a good thing, no matter what their age. What Arthur and Kathryn began still lives on across the United States and in many countries around the world.

Did You Know? Hollywood's Use of Vernacular Dance

Films use vernacular dance in many ways and for many purposes. It might set the time frame, it might cement relationships in the story line, and it might be used for the sheer entertainment factor. The steps of the vernacular or social dances were and still are often used as a basis for movement; these movements were added to, expanded on, stylized, and sometimes sanitized in Hollywood. Dance is a social equalizer. To gain an understanding about how Hollywood handles vernacular dance, view one or all of the following videos: *That's Entertainment, That's Dance,* and *Gotta Dance.*

CHAPTER 7

Review

Name _____ Class _____ Date _____

True/False

1. There was a time when humans didn't dance. _____

2. Dance occurred in ancient times. _____

3. The Greeks in ancient times performed their dances in their homes. _____

4. Tapestries that tell us about dance were prominent in the 1990s. _____

5. For social entertainment, Native Americans integrated dance and drumming into the very fabric of their lives. _____

6. Vernacular dance has no connection to the music of the day. _____

7. The black bottom dance of the Roaring Twenties was considered shocking. _____

Short Answers

1. In many cultures dance is a way to celebrate. How is it documented?

2. Who was the founder of a cultural dance company for which she had dancers trained in classical forms?

3. Cave drawings give us the sense that dance was an essential part of everyday life. What reasons were there to dance?

4. How do we know that ancient nations such as Egypt had dance as part of their culture?

5. What dance critic, historian, and lecturer who has edited hundreds of books on dance, dancers, choreographers, dance criticism, and dance history edited an all-encompassing work in the six-volume *International Encyclopedia of Dance: A Project of Dance Perspectives?*

6. Who was Arthur Murray's dance partner?

7. What are some of the ways in which films use dance?

Miniproject

Compile a costume file. When you work with the three lessons in this chapter you will come across the dress of the times. Photocopy or make drawings of the pictures, renderings, or details you found in your research. This will be the start of a minifile for you. Be sure to label each picture with the time period and country (and dance if they are doing it).

Assembling the Tools: Creating Dances

▶▶▶▶▶▶▶▶▶▶▶▶▶▶▶▶▶▶▶▶▶▶

▶▶▶▶▶▶▶▶▶▶▶▶▶▶▶▶▶▶

▶▶▶▶▶▶▶▶▶▶▶▶▶▶▶▶▶▶

From chapter 8 you will

1. learn to use the elements of choreography;

2. learn how dance-making processes enhance and carry the dance forward; and

3. be able to put your dance into a form (structure).

►Overture

Just as a building has a frame, a dance should have a choreographic structure to organize and support the main idea. Think of the choreographic processes as the hallways that take you from room to room and from floor to floor. The choreographic elements keep the dancers, the movement, and the audience's attention focused on the main idea. Choreographic elements can be used to embellish the main idea just as plaster fills in the frame and adds texture and ornamentation to the walls.

►LESSON 8.1

Dance-Making Elements

5,6,7,8 Move It!

With your classmates, brainstorm lists of loco-motor (traveling) and nonlocomotor (non-traveling) movements. On your own, choose movements from both of these lists and add shapes (angular, straight, curving, twisted, symmetrical, asymmetrical), elevation steps (jump, hop, leap, assemblé, sissonne), and falls to make a dance phrase. Videotape your dance phrase.

Vocabulary

shape • elevation • fall • facing • formation • symmetrical • asymmetrical • weight sharing • unison • focal point • tempo

Curtain Up

Dance-making, or choreographic, elements can be divided into three categories. Certain elements can be used to organize the dancers. Others can be used to manipulate movement, and certain elements can be used to guide the audience's attention. These tools give a dance a design and add interest and variety to the movement.

Dancers can be organized in various ways. The number of people dancing at one time can change the looks of a dance phrase. A dance (or section of a dance) can be a solo, duet, trio, quartet, quintet, and so on, or an ensemble. Just by changing the facings, or the stage direc-tions (downstage, upstage, stage right, stage left, diagonal) to which the dancers perform their movement, a choreographer can make even the simplest phrase more interesting. Formations, or groupings (where the dancers stand in relationship to other dancers), can be either symmetrical (even on both sides) or

► Dancers can make symmetrical and asymmetrical shapes.

asymmetrical (uneven). Four dancers could be placed in a square formation with two dancers on each side of center stage (symmetrical) or with three dancers separate from the fourth (asymmetrical). These two formations already bring to mind very different scenarios. Partnering and weight sharing (guiding and giving and taking weight from another dancer) can be used to organize dancers into various relationships in a dance.

Movement can be developed and changed through various methods. All dancers could dance in unison, doing the same movement at the same time. A gesture, movement, or dance phrase could either take on significance or lose meaning by use of repetition. Using different types (varieties) of movements or steps keeps the dance from becoming monotonous. Both literal (real-life) movements and abstract (movement that differs from but is still loosely based on the literal movement) can be used within a dance. Abstract movement is actually symbolic

of the real-life movement. You can alter certain movements just by changing the level (high, middle, low) at which they are performed. Simply by changing the size (small or large) of a movement, you can maintain the audience's interest and even change the movement's meaning. Changes in tempo, or speed, can vary the look and intent of a movement. Floor patterns, and air patterns, or imaginary patterns left behind a dancer's movements, can guide other dancers' movements in the space.

The choreographer is responsible for guiding the audience's attention during the performance. Two tools for this job are focal point (where the audience looks) and silence (stillness). If an ensemble of dancers is slowly moving around a solo dancer who is performing a percussive, fast-paced movement, at whom will the audience look? The solo dancer is the focal point. Likewise, silence can draw an audience's attention if contrasted with movement (McGreevy-Nichols et al. 2001).

Take the Stage

When you add movement to a dance phrase, you get a dance composition. Adding to a dance composition, you get a dance study. Adding to a dance study, you have a dance.

1. Review and practice the dance phrase from this lesson's Move It! Use the videotape to review it.

2. Combine your dance phrase with one or two other students' dance phrases.

Have this combined dance phrase videotaped.

3. Review the rubric on page 101 for evaluating your choreography so that you will know what the expectations are.

4. Choose movement skills and choreographic elements to develop your dance phrase into a dance composition. Make sure that you choose items from each category.

Take the Stage: Handout

Movement Skills

[ ] balance   [ ] fall and recovery   [ ] isolation   [ ] weight shift

Locomotor Movements

[ ] walk or run   [ ] slide   [ ] jump   [ ] hop   [ ] leap

[ ] assemblé (jump from one foot to two feet)   [ ] sissonne (jump from two feet to one foot)

[ ] skip   [ ] gallop   [ ] other movement from your brainstorm (list them here):

Nonlocomotor Movements

[ ] bend   [ ] twist   [ ] stretch   [ ] swing

[ ] other movement from your brainstorm (list them here):

Choreographic Elements

Organizing Dancers

[ ] solo   [ ] duet   [ ] trio   [ ] ensemble   [ ] facings   [ ] formations   [ ] symmetrical formations

[ ] asymmetrical formations   [ ] partnering and weight sharing

Manipulating Movements

[ ] unison   [ ] repetition   [ ] variety   [ ] abstract movements   [ ] literal movements   [ ] levels

[ ] size of movements   [ ] tempo changes   [ ] floor patterns   [ ] air patterns

Guiding Audience's Attention

[ ] focal point   [ ] silence (stillness)

LESSON 8.1

Take the Stage: Rubric

Rubric

(+): Dance composition includes at least nine movement skills and at least nine choreographic elements. Dance composition is well memorized and performed with concentration and complete confidence.

(√): Dance composition includes at least 8 movement skills and 8 choreographic elements. Dance composition is memorized and performed with no breaks in performance.

(–): Dance composition includes fewer than seven movement skills and fewer than seven choreographic elements and/or they are not clearly demonstrated in the composition. Performance of dance composition has two or more breaks in the performance.

From *Experiencing Dance: From Student to Dance Artist* by H. Scheff, M. Sprague, and S. McGreevy-Nichols, 2005, Champaign, IL: Human Kinetics.

 Take a Bow

The following three steps have you viewing, comparing, reflecting, and recording your work. These continue to be very important parts of assessing your work.

1. Videotape the final version of your dance composition from lesson 8.1 Take the Stage.

2. Compare this dance composition with your original dance phrase from lesson 8.1 Move It! and the combined dance phrase.

3. Describe in a paragraph or in a class discussion how including movement skills and choreographic elements improved your dance composition.

 Spotlight: David Parsons

Reprinted, by permission, from Thirteen/WNET, (New York: Educational Broadcasting Corporation). www.pbs.org/wnet/egg/203/caught/index.html.

David Parsons is the founder and artistic director of the Parsons Dance Company. Born in Illinois and raised in Kansas City, Missouri, this performer, choreographer, teacher, director, and producer of dance has created more than 60 works for the company. From 1978 to 1987 Mr. Parsons was a leading dancer with the Paul Taylor Dance Company. Parsons comments on Taylor's influence on him in an interview for the PBS series "EGG: The Arts Show:"

Working with Paul Taylor for many years, you realize he pushed himself into different places that made him uncomfortable. He would get comfy doing classical music, and then he would switch to elevator music. And I learned that I sponged up what this man did you know, he's a genius and I realized that if you really want to do something different, you have to be a little uncomfortable. And if you look at it in the real world, like the Beatles incredibly diverse, the music they used, the lyrics, the sounds, going to India and getting a sitar. Who is another example? Picasso! Great example of diversity throughout his career, the blue period I mean it's totally different than Cubism and his early drawings. These artists inspire me because I see them constantly changing. Madonna, now, she's constantly re-evaluating how she wants to be perceived, or how she wants her work to look because that's excitement. Change!

Did You Know? David Parsons Video

Interested in watching David Parsons work? Produced as part of a public television series, the video *Behind the Scenes With David Parsons* (1992) focuses on the process that Parsons used to create the piece *Sleep Study*. Working with dancers from American Ballet Theatre, Parsons explains the creative process that he used to develop a dance sequence based on how people move while sleeping. You can shop for this video online at major bookstores.

Dance-Making Processes

5,6,7,8 Move It!

Have a movement conversation with a partner. (Remember that in a conversation one person speaks while the other listens and vice versa.) In responding to your partner, use opposite (contrasting) movement when disagreeing; repeat (copy) your partner's movement when agreeing; add similar (complementary) movement when wishing to extend the comment; and repeat and add short transitional moves when you want your partner to add on to her or his original comment.

Vocabulary

choreographic processes • transition • contrast • copy • complementary • call and response

Curtain Up

Choreographic processes are methods used to enhance and carry the dance forward.

- A transition is movement that connects one movement or dance phrase to the next movement or movement phrase. For example, if you have a movement at low level followed by a movement at high level you can make a transition through the middle level (see illustration on page 71 in chapter 6).

- Contrast adds interest through the development of opposite shapes, movements, or dance phrases. A high movement would be contrasted by a low movement.

- Copying is duplicating a shape, movement, or dance phrase. It involves moving as if you are another person's shadow, exactly replicating his movement.

- Complementary describes different but related shapes, movement, or dance phrases. An example is making a similar shape in a different direction from another shape.

► Choreographic processes can include (a) high and low contrasting shapes, (b) same shapes or copying, and (c) complementary shapes.

 Take the Stage

Choreography is a building process. The following gives you additional ways to grow your dance composition.

1. Review your dance composition that you made for lesson 8.1 Take the Stage.

2. Add transition, copy, contrast, and complementary choreographic processes to your developing dance composition.

3. Videotape your dance composition.

Take a Bow

The following three steps have you viewing, comparing, reflecting, and recording your work, which continue to be important parts of assessing your work.

1. View the video of your new dance composition and compare it to the lesson 8.1 composition.

2. Share your dance composition with the rest of the class. As you watch the other students, identify the four choreographic processes as they appear in the dances.

3. Write about or discuss with your class how adding choreographic processes changed your dance composition.

Spotlight: Tap Challenge

Tap challenge is America's answer to call and response. "The challenge dance is an African tradition in which dancers compete with each other to be the best. It has also become one of the oldest, most popular forms of rhythm tap," according to author Anne E. Johnson (1999, p. 15). Someone starts the challenge with an original rhythmic pattern. Those that challenge the movement embellish this pattern with syncopated and added rhythms that still fit the original pattern. In this way tap challenges relate to the choreographic process because they're complementary. Tap dance challenges can happen on street corners, in a studio, and on a stage. It usually takes the form of several tappers standing in a circle. One enters the middle of the circle and does a rhythmical sequence of steps with an intricate, percussive pattern. The others stand around, sometimes clapping in accompaniment or stamping a foot to the basic beat. The center dancer finishes and challenges the next dancer to come to the center and mimic the dance sequence, encouraging an enlargement of the original tap sequence. This dancer might bend forward to change the shape of the movement. This adds contrast. As they go from the circle to the center they shuffle, chug, and jump, making transitions between the challenge steps.

An added dimension is when a drummer or percussionist creates the beat and rhythm, and the dancers have to match footwork to the percussion beat and rhythm. This exercise can be raised to a fevered pitch. "Old timers" who brought this practice to an art form were Jimmy Slyde (who sometimes challenged with Buddy Rich on drums), Charles Honi Coles, and Bunny Briggs. This exercise is often called a duel, with complementary and contrasting movements shaping the choreography. In more recent years we have been treated to Gregory Hines' challenging Savion Glover.

▶ "Anything you can do, I can do better!"

Did You Know? Tap Improvisation

How did the dancers mentioned in lesson 8.2 Spotlight build their knowledge and choreography when they had no formal dance training? They learned their craft and handed it on in many different ways. The rhythms of a tap challenge were part of improvisation. They made them up as they went along. They learned from each other "feet to feet." With each passing of the challenge, the steps got more difficult and more intricate. The observers, many of them young, caught on to what the performers in the circle were doing, and thus the challenge steps were handed down to the next generation. Not only did they learn the challenge steps and style, but each new generation of dancers incorporated its own style that was influenced by the popular music and dance of their time.

Sammy Davis Jr., Gregory Hines, and the Nicholas Brothers were unlike other tappers because they had formal training. They added to that formal training by turning to the masters that came before them. Dancers still enter challenges. They engage in "tap jams" and festivals.

You can search the Internet to learn about tap, tap jam sessions, and festivals. Some key words are "tap," "hoofers," "tap challenge," "Savion Glover," "Gregory Hines," "Fred Astaire," and "tap dance improvisation."

You can find more information about tap from the following sources:

- Frank, Rusty E. 1990. *Tap! The greatest tap dance stars and their stories 1900–1955.* New York: William Morrow.

- Johnson, Anne E. 1999. *Jazz tap: From African drums to American feet.* New York: Rosen.

Dance-Making Structures

5,6,7,8 Move It!

Create a dance phrase to represent the lyrics of "Row, Row, Row Your Boat" or "Frere Jacques." A duet or trio performs the dance phrase in a four-count canon, the way that the songs are usually sung. Just as the same lyrics and melodies are sung at four-count intervals, a movement canon requires that the same movement be done at specified intervals. In this case, the dancers should start the dance phrase four counts apart.

Vocabulary

AB • ABA • ground bass • canon • rondo • collage • accumulation • chance dance • motif and development • narrative • theme • variation

Curtain Up

"Once you have developed material (dance movements and dance phrases), you will need to organize it within some type of structure" (McGreevy-Nichols et al. 2001, p. 25). The following explains the various types of structures commonly used for choreography. In some instances they bear great similarity to musical structures (McGreevy-Nichols et al. 2001, p. 25).

- A canon, also known as a round, is two or more movement parts involved in a composition in which the main movement is imitated exactly and completely by the successive movements, but the different parts are staggered. It is the equivalent of singing "Row, Row, Row Your Boat" in staggered parts but using movement in place of the words.
- The AB format can be described as A, a dance phrase, and B, a new dance phrase.
- The ABA format can be described as A, a dance phrase, B, a new dance phrase, and a return to A, the first dance phrase.
- A rondo can be described as ABACADA. The choreographic pattern begins with a main theme (A) followed by another theme or movement material, and the A theme returns after each new movement phrase.
- Theme and variation format can be described as a dance phrase or section of a dance with subsequent dance phrases or sections being variations of the original. This would be A, A1, A2, A3.
- The narrative choreographic form tells a story or conveys an idea. The sequence of the story determines the structure of the dance.
- Collage is a choreographic form that "consists of a series of movement phrases that are often unrelated but have been brought together to create a single dance with a beginning, a middle, and an end" (McGreevy-Nichols et al. 2001, p. 25).
- Accumulation is a choreographic form that can be described by the following model: (1), (1,2), (1,2,3), (1,2,3,4), (1,2,3,4,5). If each number represents a distinct movement or dance phrase, then it is clear that "this structure is constructed by adding on different movement or dance phrases" (McGreevy-Nichols et al. 2001, p. 25).
- Call and response as a choreographic form can be described as conversational:

Theme

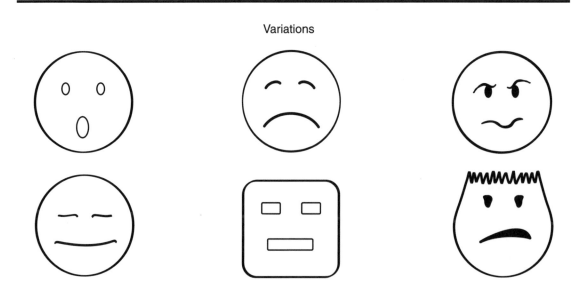

Variations

One person moves and the other person's movement responds to (answers) the movement of the initial mover, just as in a tap challenge.

- Chance dance as a choreographic form can be described as a "series of dance phrases performed in a random order. Each time the dance is done, it is in a different order and therefore has a different appearance" (McGreevy-Nichols et al. 2001, p. 25).

- Motif and development as a choreographic form can be described as "a brief movement phrase that is danced then developed into a full blown dance or section of a dance" (McGreevy-Nichols et al. 2001, p. 25).

- Suite as a choreographic form "uses different tempos and qualities in its three or more sections" (McGreevy-Nichols et al. 2001, p. 25). Usually the first section is a moderate tempo, the second is an adagio (slow tempo), and the last section is an allegro (fast tempo).

- Beginning, middle, and end are basic to all the choreographic structures listed previously. A dance should have a beginning shape or pose or entrance, a middle consisting of development or exploration of the main idea, and a clear ending consisting of a shape or pose or exit.

- Ground bass is like the backup singers in a singing group. A group of dancers repeats a series of simple movements while, in front, fewer dancers (or a soloist) perform a contrasting, often more complex dance phrase.

LESSON 8.3

Curtain Up: Chance Dance

The following symbols represent small dance phrases that can be the inspiration for a chance dance. When different phrases are learned, it becomes fun and a challenge for the phrases to be mixed up to create different-looking dances.

Sequence A

Sequence B

Sequence C

Take the Stage

By doing the following activity, you and your peers will have a better understanding of choreographic form.

1. Choose a choreographic form at random.

2. With your partner, decide where the choreographic form would best fit in your dance composition that you developed in lesson 8.2 Take the Stage. Should the whole dance be used to demonstrate the form, or should a smaller section or dance phrase be used?

3. Using the explanations in lesson 8.3 Curtain Up, select a choreographic form to organize your dance composition.

LESSON 8.3

Take the Stage: Choreographic Forms

AB	**ABA**
MOTIF & DEVELOPMENT	**THEME & VARIATION**
RONDO	**CANON**
COLLAGE	**GROUND BASS**
ACCUMULATION	**CALL & RESPONSE**

Take a Bow

The following two steps have you viewing, comparing, reflecting, and recording your work. These continue to be an important part of assessing your work.

1. Perform the dance composition for the class, and have it videotaped. Have your peers use the illustrated rubric to evaluate your work.

2. Using the videotapes, compare and contrast all three versions of this dance composition. Write in your journal or discuss in your class how the choreographic elements, processes, and forms changed and improved your dance composition.

Spotlight: Merce Cunningham

Merce Cunningham (1919-), one of America's pioneers in modern dance, is known for his avant-garde approach to choreography. His early training with Martha Graham's company and his friendship with John Cage, the piano accompanist in Graham's classes, led to the creation of his roles in pieces such as *Letter to the World* and *Every Soul Is a Circus,* some of Graham's signature works. After two additional years of study at the American School of the Ballet and an intensive personal exploration of movement techniques, Cunningham began shaping a nonlinear approach to movement. He rejected a position in Graham's company and a solo role in Agnes de Mille's Broadway-bound musical *One Touch of Venus* to pursue his own experiments.

Renowned for doing the unusual, Cunningham is always pushing the envelope. One of the approaches that he uses in creating choreography is referred to as *chance dance.* Chance dance, now a well-known choreographic structure, involves creating dances based on chance arrangements.

"Instead of using the phrasing of the music to dictate the movement, they used the idea of 'chance'—music, design, and movement composed completely independently of each other. He wanted dance to be 'itself,' eliminating the idea of narrative and enabling the audience to make their own interpretations. Cunningham's aim was to educate people away from this concern for narrative, which he felt stifled creativity" (theatremuseum.vam.ac.uk/placecunn.htm).

The arrangements could be decided by a flip of the coin, the audience, or an arbitrary shuffling of the sequences. To find out more information about Merce Cunningham, do a Web search using the following key words: "Merce Cunningham," "chance dance," "pioneers in modern dance," "choreographers," and "Merce Cunningham Dance Company."

Did You Know? John Cage

There is a school of thought that believes that dance and music do not necessarily have to relate to each other. They think that both can be performed at the same time. The two can exist separately but are equal. John Cage (1912-1992), known for his eclectic music compositions, started collaborating with Merce Cunningham in 1943. In an autobiographical statement, Cage comments, "In our collaborations Merce Cunningham's choreographies are not supported by my musical accompaniments. Music and dance are independent but coexistent." (Adapted from *John Cage: An Autobiographical Statement,* www.newalbion.com/artists/cagej/autobiog.html.)

In 1991 the CD *Cage: Music for Merce Cunningham, volume 4* became the first audio document of the collaboration between Cage and Cunningham. Interested in finding out more about John Cage? Visit a local music store to check out some of his musical creations.

CHAPTER 8

Review

Name _____ Class _____ Date _____

True/False

1. Choreographic processes are methods used to enhance and carry the dance forward. _____

2. Merce Cunningham, one of America's pioneers in modern dance, is known for his classical approach to choreography. _____

3. The number of people dancing at one time can change the look of a dance phrase. _____

4. The choreographer is not responsible for guiding the audience's attention during the performance of a dance. _____

5. Tap challenge is America's answer to call and response. _____

6. Stillness (silence) can draw an audience's attention if contrasted with movement. _____

7. Sammy Davis Jr., Gregory Hines, and the Nicholas Brothers had no formal dance training. _____

Short Answers

1. What is a transition?

2. What composer collaborated with Merce Cunningham?

3. Name four types of structures commonly used for choreography.

4. What company did David Parsons dance with before breaking out on his own?

5. Name three old-timers who perfected the craft of tap challenge.

6. What does the dance term *complementary* describe?

7. What is chance dance?

Devising a Dance Tool Kit

Collect all the dance skills and elements and choreographic elements and structures that you have learned about. Make a kit of cards to have as a handy reference when you begin choreographing.

Crafting Your Dance: Choreography

▶▶▶▶▶▶▶▶▶▶▶▶▶▶▶▶▶▶

▶▶▶▶▶▶▶▶▶▶▶▶▶▶▶▶

From chapter 9 you will

1. complete a seven-step method for creating a dance;

2. learn how to generate dance movement from any inspiration; and

3. learn how to choose and chart music and enhance your choreography with movement elements and choreographic elements.

►Overture

Like any other process, choreography has a logical progression. This series of steps through the choreographic process demystifies the making of a dance. Think of choreography as a step-by-step process, building a staircase to the top. From beginning to end you are the creator, you fill in the blanks, you reap the rewards. How rewarding it is to see an idea that began in your mind become something for others to see and appreciate. A seven-step method for the choreographic process will be spread out over the three lessons in this chapter. Have a great time—5-6-7-8!

Choose Subject Matter, Explore Movement

5,6,7,8 Move It!

You can dance about anything. Even the simplest ideas can become great works of art. As a class, improvise (make up on the spot without any forethought) movement based on the idea of meeting up with someone, greeting this person, and leaving her. Continue with this idea as you meet, greet, and leave other classmates. Do not become too literal (real) with your movement. Challenge yourself to stay in the dance mode. Find different movement for each meeting.

Vocabulary

improvise • literal movement • abstract movement

Curtain Up

When you choreograph a dance, you can follow seven simple steps. (All seven steps are from McGreevy-Nichols et al. 2001.) If you follow these steps and the Choreography Project Checklist in this lesson's Take a Bow, you will have both an interesting dance and clear documentation of your work (your choreographic process).

Step 1: Choose subject matter—the inspiration. The inspiration or idea is the foundation on which a choreographer builds a dance. It is your subject matter. As in good writing, anything can become a thesis. So, too, a dance can be made about a story; a piece of music; poetry; or a theme from history, science, or math. As you come across different inspirations, write them in a personal journal or save them in a recipe box or file folder. As you need ideas for choreography, you will be able to make a choice from this collection.

Step 2: Explore and select movements—inventing movement. After choosing an inspiration, invent or explore movement. This exploration can be approached in a variety of ways. Words such as verbs, especially the action words, will easily lend themselves to movement. Descriptive words, such as adverbs and adjectives, will help you color your movement with the appropriate expressive qualities for the clearest communication of your ideas. Of course, more traditional research methods will give you much information for your dance making. Use dictionaries, interviews, the Internet, poetry indexes, books, videotapes, and any other resource to develop an understanding of your topic.

Movement can be invented and explored by the use of improvisation. Improvisation is playing with movement. Movement begets movement. One simple movement can multiply itself. Do a movement, and repeat it if you have to until another movement flows out of it. Before you know it, you will have invented a dance phrase. A dance phrase can be likened to a sentence. Dance sentences can be combined or developed into a movement paragraph or section of a dance.

Often, during the exploration phase, especially if you are beginning by generating movement from words, movements can be very literal. Changing this literal movement into abstract (symbolic) movement will help you develop more original and interesting movement material.

This abstract movement has within it the essential qualities, or seed, of the initial literal movement. The popcorn analogy illustrates the difference between literal and abstract movement. Unpopped popcorn is kernels of corn. After it is popped, it becomes big and fluffy. Despite its appearance, though, it is still corn! Using the literal handshake movement as an example, following are some suggestions for transforming it into abstract or symbolic movement (McGreevy-Nichols et al. 2001, p. 20):

- Change the rhythm. For example, make the rhythm of the handshake uneven (instead of only going up and down, shake up, up, up, down).

- Change or vary the speed. For example, shake hands very slowly, then extremely fast.

- Change or vary the size of the movement. For example, make the handshake so small that you can barely see it, and so large you have to move from a high to a low level.

- Repeat the movement over and over. For example, repeat the movement until it loses its significance as a gesture and becomes simply a movement.

- Use the same movement with a different body part. For example, do the handshake movement with your elbow, foot, or head.

- Do the opposite action and combine it with the original movement. For example, instead of facing the person you are greeting, move away as if to ignore the other person.

- Make a new unrelated movement and mix it in with the original movement. For example, spin on your toes and connect it with the handshake.

- Interrupt or have the movement take a detour to augment the original movement. For example, begin to shake hands, then use a locomotor movement to travel away, and finally return to finish the handshake.

- Let the movement grow and change. For example, repeat the handshake until it starts to change, and follow it wherever it may lead.

► During a movement phrase, movements can be *(a)* literal, *(b)* semiabstract, or *(c)* very abstract, such as these clocks.

 Take the Stage

This activity will help you choose the inspiration for your dance from a myriad of possibilities. (A choreographer must narrow many options to the final choice.) It will also help you do some form of research and begin to explore movements appropriate to your inspiration.

1. As you see, feel, hear, experience, and think of ideas and inspirations for dances, write them in your inspiration journal. Be sure to explain why this inspiration or idea might make a good dance. (If you are creating a dance with a small group, share these ideas with your choreography project team members.)

2. Choose three of your favorite ideas or inspirations to explore.

3. Make a tiny dance phrase on each idea, and videotape each of them.

4. Look at a video of your dance phrases, and choose your favorite idea or inspiration. Make sure that you (and your group) love this idea or inspiration, because it will be the basis for your whole dance.

5. Use some form of research to deepen your understanding of your topic. Choose some main ideas from this research to be used for sections of your dance.

6. Consider the qualities that would best express these main ideas. Use them along with improvisation to make up dance phrases for each section.

 Take a Bow

Document your thinking and work for this lesson's Take the Stage by completing tasks 1, 2, 3, 4, and 5.1 in your Choreography Project Checklist. The Choreography Project Checklist on the following page will function as documentation of your work. It will also walk you through the choreographic process. The Choreography Project Checklist includes rubrics. Some are for teacher evaluation, and some are for self-evaluation and peer evaluation. In any case, the rubrics should be used to guide your work.

Take a Bow: Student Choreography Project Checklist Part I

Name _____ Class _____ Date _____

Rubric

(This checklist will be weighed 5 times your score. Teacher evaluates the work using this rubric.)

(5) = All items of the checklist are completed and filled out; descriptions and explanations contain much helpful information.

(4) = All items of the checklist are completed and filled out.

(3) = Fewer than three items are left blank.

(2) = Four to six items are left blank.

(1) = Checklist shows very little evidence of student work in the project.

(0) = No effort is shown.

Task 1. Names of people in your choreography group:

Rubric

(Teamwork Evaluation for whole choreography project: work cooperatively in a small group during the choreographic process. To be completed by all members of the choreography project team at the completion of the project. Use the peer teamwork evaluation form. Total results of the evaluations are recorded here by teacher.)

(5) = All peer teamwork evaluations are above standard.

(4) = Most of peer teamwork evaluations are at standard.

(3) = Fewer than half of peer teamwork evaluations are at standard.

(2) = Most of peer teamwork evaluations are below standard.

(1) = All of peer teamwork evaluations are below standard.

Task 2. List two or three interesting ideas from inspiration journal and brainstorming exercise. (Attach all the inspiration journals to your group's choreography folder.)

Due date: _____

Task 3. After exploring movements for each of the ideas listed previously and watching the videotape, we chose to choreograph a dance about . . .

because . . .

Teacher's signature: _____ Date: _____   *(continued)*

Task 4. Research.

4.1 We got information on this idea by using the following sources:

Books: (1)

(2)

Movement improvisations and explorations: (Date of videotaping: _____)

Interviews with the following people:

Videotapes:

Other sources:

Rubric

(Teacher uses rubric to evaluate.)

(5) = More than one type of research source is used. All notes are put into the team's choreography folder. Resources are cited appropriately. Research is clearly used in the choreography.

(4) = All notes are put into the team's choreography folder. Resources are listed. Research is clearly used in the choreography.

(3) = Some evidence of research is put into the choreography folder, and/or not all resources are listed, and/or research is not clearly visible in choreography.

(2) = Very little evidence of research is put into the choreography folder, and/or resources are not listed, and/or research is not used in choreography.

(1) = Some research is done (teacher observation), but no evidence of research or use of research is apparent.

(0) = No attempt at research was made.

Teacher's signature:: _____ Date: _____

 From *Experiencing Dance: From Student to Dance Artist* by H. Scheff, M. Sprague, and S. McGreevy-Nichols, 2005, Champaign, IL: Human Kinetics.

4.2 List the main ideas that you got out of the research that you plan to use for your dance.

Teacher's signature: _____ Date: _____

Task 5. Making movement material for your dance.

5.1 List the main sections of the dance and brainstorm images and qualities that you see or feel in your imagination.

    1.

    2.

    3.

    4.

Teacher's signature: _____ Date: _____

Spotlight: Jawole Willa Jo Zollar

Jawole Willa Jo Zollar (1950-) founded Urban Bush Women in 1984, a dance company whose basis for style and material is religious traditions and folklore of the African diaspora. With her company and collaborators from other fields, she creates a sense of community on stage through her dance themes. She often works with writers, other dancers or choreographers, and musicians. Ms. Zollar's credentials include a BA in dance from the University of Missouri at Kansas City, an MFA from Florida State, two Inter-Arts grants, and three Choreographer's Fellowships from the National Endowment for the Arts.

Jawole Willa Jo Zollar's works include "Song of Lawino" (1988), "I Don't Know, But I've Been Told, If you Keep on Dancin' You'll Never Grow Old" (1989), and "Praise House" (1990). (Malone 2003)

Did You Know? Passing On Choreography

Apprentices learn from master craftspersons, or experts. In the same way, young choreographers should learn from master choreographers. If it is difficult for you to go to many professional dance concerts, then the next best thing is to use videotaped performances. As you work with inspirations, a good resource is the videotape of *Modest Mussorgsky: Pictures at an Exhibition* (1992), choreographed by Moses Pendleton.

This dance is actually made up of many smaller dances. Each section is based on a different inspiration. A character, sometimes the conductor and sometimes the choreographer, acts as a transition between each section by walking and looking at different paintings that represent the inspirations. Watch, imagine, enjoy, and analyze this masterful dance. (Your teacher may give you a viewing guide to help you analyze this piece. This viewing guide will help you identify the inspirations for the different sections of the dance. It will also help you identify choreographic and movement elements used in each section.)

Coordinate Music and Movement, Explore Possibilities, Refine, and Memorize

5,6,7,8 **Move It!**

Design a small dance phrase. Choose some music. Set your dance phrase to the music selection. Show the dance phrase to peers with and without the music. Ask them which version they liked best.

Vocabulary

muscle memory • accented beats

Curtain Up

Musical accompaniment should add to the effectiveness of your dance. Learning how to chart the music will help you to organize your dance to fit the music. This lesson includes this information, plus some information about practicing.

Step 3: Coordinate music and movement—outlining and organizing. Music can help clarify movement and emotional qualities. It can even be an additional source of inspiration for movement.

The structure of the music could be used to organize the movement. For instance, if a canon occurs in your music, you may want to organize a dance phrase into canon form. If the music has a chorus and verse organization, you may wish to create movement that is repeated every time the chorus occurs. You may have to add, subtract, or rearrange the movement to fit the music organization. To make the structure of the music visible, the choreographer who doesn't have or can't read a musical score may wish to make his or her own chart. Music can be charted either by using the lyrics or counting the beats.

Before we go on to an explanation of charting music, first we will share an anecdote. We once used slashes (/) to represent the measures of music (4 or 8 beats or counts for each slash). In music the term *bar* is also used. We thought that our system was fairly clear. In a class of English as a Second Language students, we demonstrated the process of charting music. These children were eight years old and had limited English language skills. At the end of the demonstration, one little girl told us that she made her eights look like 8, not like /. We took her advice to heart and revised our system. For a measure with four counts, we represent it with the numeral 4. If we want to express eight counts, we represent it with the numeral 8. It makes reading the chart so much easier.

The following is an example of music outlined using the lyrics for "Jack and Jill" (McGreevy-Nichols et al., 2001, p. 21):

Jack and Jill

Phrase dance beat:

1. Jack (1) and Jill (2) went up (3) the hill (4)
2. To fetch (1) a pail (2) of wa- (3) ter (4)
3. Jack (1) fell down (2) and broke (3) his crown (4)
4. And Jill (1) came tum- (2) bling af- (3) ter (4)

Next is an example of organizing music by counting the beats.

Any Popular Song

Intro	8 8 8 8 (32 counts)
Theme A	8 8 8 8 8 (40 counts)
Theme B	8 8 8 8 (32 counts)
Transition	8 4 (12 counts)
Theme C	8 8 8 8 (32 counts for the chorus)
Theme A	8 8 8 8 8 (40 counts)
Theme B	8 8 8 8 (32 counts)
Transition	8 4 (12 counts)
Theme C	8 8 8 8 (32 counts for the chorus)
Theme D	8 8 8 8 8 8 8 8 8 8 8 8 (96 counts)
Theme A	8 8 8 8 8 (40 counts, including a fade)

Step 4: Explore possibilities—experimenting with movement components. Choreography can be enhanced by changing or adding certain components. A successful dance will keep the audience interested. Choreographers are in charge of surprising the audience with unique organizations and variations of movements. For example, you could change the rhythm of the movement by accenting different beats within each measure. (An accented beat is the beat with the heavy emphasis). Alternating the accented beat would feel like this: [**1**, 2, 3, 4] [1, **2**, 3, 4] [1, 2, **3**, 4] [1, 2, 3, **4**].

You could also change or add any of the movement skills, movement qualities, movement elements (Laban efforts; see chapter 11), effort elements (Laban effort actions, see chapter 11), choreographic structures (see lesson 8.3), choreographic processes (see lesson 8.2), and choreographic elements (see lesson 8.1). Any of these components can be used to manipulate movement and develop the dance phrases into dances. Choreographic structures, processes, and elements provide possible ways to organize your dance material and add interest to your choreography.

Step 5: Refine and memorize choreography—practice, practice, practice! In this step you and your dancers should be performing the choreography as set. Performers must be faithful to both the original inspiration and any revisions. Rehearsing can help protect against stage fright. After you practice movement many times, muscle memory takes over. That is, your nervous and muscular systems will develop a type of memory. Conscious thought is not involved; the movement just happens. Muscle memory can override nervousness. What makes for an effective rehearsal? Practice transitions (movement within and between dance sections). Be very careful not to practice any incorrect patterns. When mistakes occur or changes need to be made, *stop*, review, and try again. Practice makes you a good performer. Practice makes a good performance.

 Take the Stage

In this activity, you will develop the main sections of your dance, select music, organize the movements, and set them in order. You will then practice your dance.

1. Using the short dance phrases that you developed in lesson 9.1 Take the Stage and the ideas for the main sections of the dance (in item 5.1 from the Choreography Project Checklist), develop sections of your dance. For each section use the Dance Ideas List handout to help you create interesting movements and organizations. After you choreograph the main sections, listen to as many selections of music as possible. When you think that you have found a couple pieces of music that fit the ideas for your dance, try out some of your movements with each piece. Make your final choice.

2. Set your dance to the music. At this point, let the music influence how you perform the movement, the structure of the dance, and any new movements you add to the dance.

3. Work with appropriate movement components such as accented beats, movement skills, movement qualities, movement elements (Laban efforts; see chapter 11), effort elements (Laban effort actions; see chapter 11), choreographic structures (see lesson 8.3), choreographic processes (see lesson 8.2), and choreographic elements (see lesson 8.1).

4. Practice! Revise! Practice! Refine!

Take the Stage: Dance Ideas List

Name _____ Class _____ Date _____

Instructions: Choose the dance ideas that express the idea, theme, or image.

Movement Skills

[ ] balances   [ ] falls and recoveries   [ ] isolations   [ ] weight shifts

Locomotor Movements

[ ] walk   [ ] hop   [ ] jump   [ ] leap   [ ] assemblé (jump from one foot to two feet)

[ ] sissonne (jump from two feet to one foot)   [ ] slide   [ ] skip   [ ] gallop

Nonlocomotor Movements

[ ] bend   [ ] twist   [ ] stretch

Movement Qualities

[ ] smooth   [ ] swing   [ ] percussive   [ ] collapse   [ ] vibratory

Movement Elements (Laban Efforts) [see chapter 11, lesson 11.1]

Weight: [ ] strength   [ ] lightness
Time: [ ] sudden   [ ] sustained
Space: [ ] direct   [ ] indirect
Flow: [ ] bound   [ ] free

Effort Elements (Laban Effort Actions) [see chapter 11, lesson 11.1]

[ ] dab   [ ] punch   [ ] float   [ ] glide   [ ] wring   [ ] press   [ ] flick   [ ] slash

Choreographic Structures

[ ] canon   [ ] collage   [ ] AB   [ ] accumulation   [ ] ABA   [ ] call and response   [ ] rondo

[ ] chance dance   [ ] theme and variations   [ ] beginning, middle, and end

[ ] narrative (sequential time line of events)   [ ] ground bass

Choreographic Processes

[ ] transition   [ ] contrast   [ ] complementary   [ ] copying

(continued)

From *Experiencing Dance: From Student to Dance Artist* by H. Scheff, M. Sprague, and S. McGreevy-Nichols, 2005, Champaign, IL: Human Kinetics.

LESSON 9.2 (CONTINUED)

Choreographic Elements

Organizing Dancers in the Dance

[ ] solo   [ ] duet   [ ] trio   [ ] ensemble   [ ] facing of dancers   [ ] formations

[ ] symmetrical shapes and formations   [ ] asymmetrical shapes and formations

[ ] partnering and weight sharing

Manipulating Movement

[ ] unison   [ ] repetition   [ ] variety   [ ] abstract movements   [ ] literal movements   [ ] levels

[ ] size of movements   [ ] changes in tempo   [ ] floor patterns   [ ] air patterns

[ ] contrasting movement or shape   [ ] complementary movement or shape

Guiding Audience's Attention

[ ] focal point   [ ] silence

From *Experiencing Dance: From Student to Dance Artist* by H. Scheff, M. Sprague, and S. McGreevy-Nichols, 2005, Champaign, IL: Human Kinetics.

 Take a Bow

Document your thinking and work by completing tasks 5.2, 6.1, 6.2, 6.3, 6.4, 7.1, 7.2, and 7.3 in your Choreography Project Checklist.

 Spotlight: Lar Lubovitch

Reprinted, by permission, from B. Murphy, *Art and network culture* (New York: The Art Council). www.artandculture.com/arts/artist?artistId=701.

Lar Lubovitch's (1943-) movement style is hard to pin to a specific form, such as ballet, jazz, and modern are all apparent in his varied choreography. Lubovitch himself makes no distinction between dance styles, and it is said that he never uses the term *modern dance* only the word *dance*. Lubovitch's first inspiration, however, is music. Independently of the music, Lubovitch creates shapes. Once the shapes evolve into short movement phrases, the choreographer searches for a relationship between shape and music, building motives, psychological structures, and simple narratives into the dance. In the final product, neither music nor movement mimics the other.

Take a Bow: Student Choreography Project Checklist
Part II

Name _____ Class _____ Date _____

5.2 List the main efforts and qualities that describe the main idea. What efforts will you use to give your dance the feeling and look that fit your main idea?

Time: [ ] sudden   [ ] sustained

Weight: [ ] strength   [ ] lightness

Space: [ ] direct   [ ] indirect

Flow: [ ] bound   [ ] free

5.3 Solve movement problems for the development of movement or dance phrases. Create one movement problem per section of your dance (see item 6).

  1. Movement problem: (movement solution: _____ date videotaped: _____)

  2. Movement problem: (movement solution: _____ date videotaped: _____)

  3. Movement problem: (movement solution: _____ date videotaped: _____)

  4. Movement problem: (movement solution: _____ date videotaped: _____)

Rubric
(Use for student self-evaluation or evaluation by teacher.)

  (5) =   At least four movement problems are written, solved, and videotaped.

  (4) =   At least two movement problems are written, solved, and videotaped.

  (3) =   Only one movement problem is written; and/or the movement problems that are written are incomplete or unclear; and/or when the movement problem is solved, it does not generate much useful movement; movement is videotaped.

  (2) =   Movement problems are attempted but all are incomplete or unclear; and/or when the movement problem is solved, it does not generate much useful movement; and/or movement is not videotaped.

  (1) =   There is a very poor attempt at writing movement problems; little understanding of the concept is shown; and/or when the movement problem is solved, it does not generate much useful movement; and/or movement is not videotaped.

  (0) =   No attempt at writing or solving movement problems is shown.

(continued)

Task 6. Organizing the dance material.

(Note: You can decide where each section or movement created by solving your movement problems fits in the dance. Does the section or movement fit in the beginning, the middle, or the end?)

6.1 Write down what you want to communicate in the following sections.

Beginning (introduction, setup of mood or theme):

Middle (exploration and development of the theme):

End (resolution):

Teacher's signature: _____ Date: _____

6.2 Check off choreographic form(s) that you will use to organize this dance.

[ ] AB   [ ] ABA   [ ] rondo   [ ] theme and variation   [ ] canon   [ ] accumulation
[ ] chance   [ ] collage   [ ] motif and development   [ ] narrative
[ ] ground bass   [ ] call and response

6.3 As you create your dance, check off the choreographic elements that you are using in your dance:

[ ] solo   [ ] duet   [ ] trio   [ ] ensemble   [ ] different facings   [ ] formations
[ ] partnering or weight sharing   [ ] symmetrical shapes and formations
[ ] asymmetrical shapes and formations   [ ] variety   [ ] repetition   [ ] abstract movements
[ ] literal movements   [ ] levels   [ ] unison   [ ] size of movements   [ ] changes in tempo
[ ] floor patterns   [ ] air patterns   [ ] focal point   [ ] silence   [ ] transitions
[ ] contrasting movements and shapes   [ ] complementary movements and shapes
Other:

    From *Experiencing Dance: From Student to Dance Artist* by H. Scheff, M. Sprague, and S. McGreevy-Nichols, 2005, Champaign, IL: Human Kinetics.

6.4 On a separate sheet of paper, draw spacing diagrams that show entrances, exits, formations, and floor patterns as seen in the following examples.

(E = enter, X = exit, T = person and facing [bottom of the T indicates where the dancer is facing; / T \ indicates that dancer is facing downstage; SR = stage right; SL = stage left.])

Examples of spacing diagrams

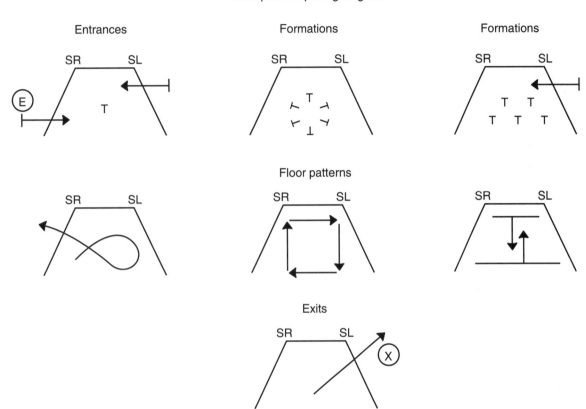

Task 7. Score or music selection.

7.1 List the different music that you listened to:

7.2 Final selection (please state the reason you chose this piece of music):

7.3 Music diagram (you may use slashes (/) or numbers to count out your music. Use commas (,) to show phrasing breaks in the music):

Teacher's signature: _____ Date: _____

From *Experiencing Dance: From Student to Dance Artist* by H. Scheff, M. Sprague, and S. McGreevy-Nichols, 2005, Champaign, IL: Human Kinetics.

Did You Know? Remy Charlip

Ready for something different? *Instructions From Paris*, by artist, children's writer, and choreographer Remy Charlip, was inspired by French postcards, sign language, and the *First Remy Charlip Reader*. Charlip would mail instructions for the dance to the dancer. The instructions would include drawings taken from French postcards and of sign language movements. He would give additional movement instructions, such as "turn," connecting the individual drawings. The dancer would then use these instructions to pull together the dance. For additional information about his other dance works or books, visit the Internet. Do a Web search using the words "Remy Charlip."

Add Finishing Touches and Perform

₅,₆,₇,₈ Move It!

Take movement from a section of your choreography or from another piece you know. Perform it for a peer with and without a piece of costuming. Together, discuss how the costuming added to or detracted from the effectiveness of the dancing. In your discussion consider the following questions: Did the costume help or hinder the dancer's movement and the concept or quality of the movement? Why or why not? What, if any, are the suggested revisions?

Vocabulary

exhibition

Curtain Up

The final two steps of your dance making are what make the process complete. While the choreographer is creating the actual dance movements and developing and shaping the final form of the dance, the fact that dance is a performing art should be constantly on the choreographer's mind. The choreographer should be asking whether the dance is communicating clearly. Other considerations relating to showcasing the dance, of course, are costumes, lights, sets, and props, our sixth step. The seventh step is always the performance itself.

Step 6: Add the finishing touches—details make a difference. A dance can only be improved through careful attention to the surrounding presentation details. During the creation of your choreography, you should also be thinking about costumes, props, set pieces, and lighting. It is your responsibility to introduce into the rehearsal process the costumes, props, and set pieces that are integral to your work. Not only do these aspects add detail and embellishment, but they can sometimes play a part in developing new and more qualitative movement as well. For example, it is easy to see how using a 15-foot length of light fabric to represent a river can be used to generate movement and staging formations. If you are considering having your dancers wear long skirts, capes, or any piece that may change how a dancer performs the choreographed movements, you should try the costume piece (or a similar practice piece) during a rehearsal. This is important not only to give the dancers time to get used to moving in the costume but also to see if you really like the way the costume fits the dance's concept. For more specific information on this step, see chapter 10.

Step 7: Perform the choreography exhibition at its best! Any performance, any time you appear before an audience of any size, is an exhibition. Steps 1 through 6 are completed. The dancers are well rehearsed and confident. The costumes, props, sets, and lighting are set.

The performance space (a formal proscenium stage or a more informal studio space) has been chosen and is ready. The audience is seated. It is now time to unveil your work. It is time to share your inspiration with others. Many positive values are associated with performing: the joy and satisfaction of creating a piece of art that has never existed before, learning about the power of dance to transport both the performer and the audience emotionally and imaginatively, and most of all, learning to love not only the product (the dance) but also the process of creating (the choreographic process).

Take the Stage

Your dance is constructed and fairly complete. This activity will help you put the finishing touches on your dance work. You may find it helpful to consult or review other chapters in this book for more detailed information.

1. Design and construct the costumes. Think about the main idea or inspiration for the dance. Consider the types of movement you have included. The costumes should not inhibit or distract from this movement. (See chapter 10 for more information.)

2. If you think that they are needed, design and construct sets and props. If you choose to use a prop, be prepared for some extra rehearsal time for the incorporation of the prop into the movement. (See chapter 10 for more information.)

3. Decide what the lighting should be. This design is dependent on the performance facility as well as the main idea or inspiration. Decide what the cues are for lighting changes. (See chapter 10 for more information.)

4. Write up the program copy.

5. Perform the final version of the dance for an audience. (See chapters 10 and 14.)

► Simple props enhance a dance.

© Bruce Davis

Take a Bow

To complete the documentation of your work, finish the last items in the checklist and review or revise all the writing in your Choreography Project Checklist.

1. Document your thinking and work by completing tasks 8.1, 8.2, 8.3, and 9 in your Choreography Project Checklist.

2. Have teachers and dancers in the audience evaluate your dance by using the rubric and assessment form.

3. Write a final report on this experience with the art of choreography.

Spotlight: Gene Kelly

Adapted from "Gene Kelly: Anatomy of a Dancer" at www.pbs.org/wnet/americanmasters/database/kelly_g.html.

"I didn't want to move or act like a rich man. I wanted to dance in a pair of jeans. I wanted to dance like the man in the streets."

Gene Kelly's (1912-1996) body of work still thrives and still thrills. With films that include *Singin' in the Rain, An American in Paris, Summer Stock, On the Town,* and *Brigadoon,* Kelly revived the movie musical and redefined dance on screen. Along with Fred Astaire he was a master of incorporating props and sets into his choreography. Some of the props and set pieces that these two gentlemen and Donald O'Connor used were trashcan lids, cartooned sets, brooms, chairs, shoes, canes and hats, sofas, and even walls and ceilings.

Kelly continued his innovative approach to material by placing himself in a cartoon environment to dance with Jerry the Mouse in *Anchors Aweigh,* yet another musical first. Determined from the start to differentiate himself from Fred Astaire, Kelly concerned himself with incorporating less ballroom dancing and more distinctly American athleticism into his choreography. *Singin' in the Rain* highlights his genius with set design and the water as he danced in the rain. Here he incorporated lampposts, water puddles, an umbrella, and the downspout from a rain gutter. He was very ill when they filmed this sequence. In 1951, he was awarded a special Oscar for *An American in Paris* for his 'extreme versatility as an actor, singer, director and dancer, but specifically for his brilliant achievement in the art of choreography.'

Take a Bow: Student Choreography Project Checklist
Part III

Name _____ Class _____ Date _____

Task 8.

8.1 Costume design (sketch or describe):

8.2 Sets and props (sketch or describe):

8.3 Lighting description:

    Q1:

    Q2:

    Q3:

    Q4:

    Q5:

(continued)

LESSON 9.3 (CONTINUED)

Task 9. Final program copy:

Title of the dance:

Choreographers and dancers:

Music:

Teacher's signature: _____ Date: _____

Did You Know? Julie Taymor and Puppets of *The Lion King*

Adapted from "Julie Taymor Enthrones 'The Lion King'" by Jackie Demaline, Cincinnati Enquirer, 2003 at www.cincinnati.com/freetime/weekend/032103_lionking.html.

Sometimes choreographers ask dancers to be part of a prop, using their bodies as extensions. When Garth Fagan signed on as choreographer for the live Broadway version of *The Lion King* he discovered that his dancers and their movements would be integrated with the puppets and props designed by Julie Taymor. These animal costumes are actually full-sized puppets, some requiring two dancers to make them function. Ms. Taymor designed these puppets with the dancer in mind so that the prop and costume animal required the dancer in it to come alive. The more than 200 creations range in size from a 5-inch mouse (not a whole dancer fits into this one) to an 18-foot giraffe. Ms. Taymor wanted humans to be a living part and to bring the beasts to life before the audience. The dancers found it difficult, at first, to dance their parts, but with plenty of rehearsal they made the magic happen. (Demaline 2003)

Take a Bow: Rubric

5 =   __ 20 or more movement skills, elements, and qualities are used for great variety and interest.

__ 23 or more choreographic forms, processes, and elements are clearly used to organize the dance.

__ Dance includes most of the following: balance, fall and recovery, isolation, weight shift, elevation, and landing.

And/or

__ The dance is complete or enough of the dance is finished to give the evaluator a sense of the completed dance.

__ Evaluator recommends this dance for the concert.

4 =   __ 16 to 19 movement skills, elements, and qualities are used for variety and interest.

__ 17 to 22 choreographic forms, processes, and elements are used to organize the dance.

__ Dance includes some of the following: balance, fall and recovery, isolation, weight shift, elevation, and landing.

And/or

__ Enough of the dance is finished to give the evaluator a sense of the completed dance.

3 =   __ 10 to 16 movement skills, elements, and qualities are used.

__ 9 to 16 choreographic forms, processes, and elements are used to organize the dance.

And/or

__ Enough of the dance is finished to give the evaluator a sense of the completed dance, but the dance needs much more revision and work.

2 =   __ Fewer than 9 movement skills, elements, and qualities are used.

__ Fewer than 8 choreographic forms, processes, and elements are clearly seen in the dance.

__ Not enough of the dance is finished to give the evaluator a sense of the completed dance.

1 =   __ Not enough of the dance is performed to allow the evaluator to grade the dance.

CHAPTER 9

Review

Name _____ Class _____ Date _____

True/False

1. The subject matter of your dance is your inspiration. _____

2. In the popcorn analogy, abstract movement is to literal movement as popcorn is to caramel corn. _____

3. Urban Bush Women get inspiration from the religious traditions and folklore of the African diaspora. _____

4. *The Lion King* uses 50 puppet costumes. _____

5. The last step in the choreographic process is performing. _____

6. Lar Lubovitch made no distinction between dance styles. _____

7. Music can be the cement that holds a dance together. _____

Short Answers

1. In the dance-making process, what do descriptive words tell you?

2. What can you do to develop an understanding of the topic of your inspiration?

3. Who choreographed *Pictures at an Exhibition*?

4. Who placed himself in a cartoon environment to dance with Jerry the Mouse in *Anchors Aweigh*?

5. How can you enhance your choreography before the performance stage?

6. What was one method that Remy Charlip used to source (gather) material for choreography?

7. What can music do for your choreography?

Project: Start a Choreographer's Log

Perhaps you have choreographed pieces before taking this class. Maybe this is your first attempt. In either case, start documenting your own work by putting what you have done on paper with your notes on how you altered (fixed) and enhanced and how you felt when you were making the additions and deletions and polishing the piece for performance.

10

Showcasing Your Work: Curtain Up, Lights On

▶▶▶▶▶▶▶▶▶▶▶▶▶▶▶▶▶▶▶

▶▶▶▶▶▶▶▶▶▶▶▶▶▶

Lesson 10.1 Costumes and Props

Lesson 10.2 Lighting, Scenery, and Sound

Lesson 10.3 Production Information and Time Line

▶▶▶▶▶▶▶▶▶▶▶▶▶▶

From chapter 10 you will

1. understand the need for dancers and choreographers to know about the technical aspects of a production;

2. become familiar with the areas of costumes, props, scenery, sound, and lighting; and

3. become knowledgeable about a production time line and the need for it.

►Overture

A good dance enhanced by a great production can be magnificent! Conversely, a bad production detracts from a good dance. Both the choreographer and the performer need to understand the components of producing a full, as well as an informal, production. Being involved in the production end of a performance is a total learning experience. It is the ultimate experience in teamwork.

►LESSON 10.1

Costumes and Props

5,6,7,8 Move It!

Costumes and props can do more than just enhance a dance. They can also inspire movement and style. Choose a costume piece or a prop. Improvise and explore movement that is inspired by the costume piece or prop. Arrange this movement into a dance composition or study. Share it with the class. (If your teacher gives you a rubric, make sure you refer to it as you work on your dance composition or study.)

Vocabulary

on the bias • tutu

Curtain Up

Think about dressing up your dance. What can you do to enhance your work? What do you have to know to work toward a complete production?

Costumes

As a choreographer producing a dance work, part of your job is to think about costumes. You may never have sewn a button on a shirt, let alone put a garment of any kind together, but think positively and keep it simple. For a dance without a story, you can select a color theme for your dancers. Ask the dancers to supply usable clothing in the necessary colors. Let's say you are staging a dance or dances about the ocean and the tides. The dancers can wear shades of blue and green with a bit of white (for the foam). If you are also representing the tides, you can use shades of color appropriate for the sun and the moon. They can wear leotards and tights, if available. They can wear T-shirts with shorts, sweat pants, or flowing skirts. They can be wrapped in flowing cloth. Never doubt the

► A sample costume sketch from costumer Ray Kahn.

versatility of fabric glue and paper and plastic, especially if it is a one-time performance.

If you are on an even tighter budget, you can look in any resale shop to find anything from skirts and shirts to pants and jackets. Remember, from a distance, the audience to the stage, the look is very different than from up close. You don't have to worry about a few worn spots or other such problems. Tiny blemishes won't spoil the illusion.

In some areas, local dance or theater companies might have a borrowing policy in which they let you borrow or rent (for a nominal fee) their costumes, provided you promise to return them in good shape and cleaned. They might even enter into an agreement in which you would donate internship hours in lieu of a rental fee. You could credit them in your program or print a notice about their next presentations (McGreevy-Nichols et al. 2001).

Props

The use of props can add a further dimension to your piece and can sometimes help reduce costume and scenery costs. Your imagination and creativity are your limit. For any flashy tune like "Puttin' On the Ritz," you can make canes by getting wide wooden dowels and painting their tops shiny white and their bottoms shiny black. For "Masquerade" from *Phantom of the Opera*, you can trim inexpensive, plain party masks with glitter, feathers, gold paint, and mock jewels. "A favorite example from *Building Dances* involves wearing a tissue box on the head. Several [dancers] wearing this prop could form the yellow brick road in the *Wizard of Oz* or the Great Wall of China. When you paint them with commonly used colors, you can reuse them" (McGreevy-Nichols et al. 2001, p. 32). One man's trash is another man's treasure, and that is the key to collecting items as props. You can think of a prop that you want to use and go look for it, or you can find a prop that will inspire your dance. Be sure to look to the art room, art students, and art teachers for ideas and materials (McGreevy-Nichols et al. 2001).

► Simple props can also act as moving scenery.

Take the Stage

Your dancers need to be clothed in costumes that are appropriate for your original inspiration. This activity will lead you through the process of designing and constructing costuming.

1. As you read through this assignment, decide which of the dance phrases or dances you created in previous chapters work best for this assignment.

2. Think about and then design (sketch) a costume or costumes that befit the piece of choreography. Remember to think about ease of movement and the whole look. Think of it in two ways: You have a very limited budget, and you have no financial constraints.

3. Construct the costume that you designed for a limited budget.

4. Rehearse and refine choreography to work with the costumes. (Do not wait until the final dress rehearsal to work with the costume.)

5. Be sure to videotape the dance without costumes and then in costume.

 Spotlight: Barbara Karinska

Madame Barbara Karinska (1888-1983) was one of the most famous and prolific costume designers for dance. She was born in Russia and worked with George Balanchine there; however, most of her work with him took place in the United States. She designed and constructed costumes for Broadway and film as well as for dance, but after 1964 her studio constructed costumes only for New York City Ballet.

Madame Karinska made two invaluable contributions to the design of ballet costumes that revolutionized how other designers would subsequently construct costumes. The first was in the design of a tutu, nicknamed the powder puff tutu.

> The tutu had no hoop, only six or seven layers of gathered net, rather than the twelve or more used for the hoop tutu. The layers, each a half inch longer than the previous one, were short, never precisely aligned but tacked together loosely giving the skirt an unprecedented softness and fullness. The skirt fell in a natural, slightly downward slope over the hips to the tops of the thighs. But the skirt was only the most obvious of the changes and details that Karinska instituted. It was her innovations with the bodice that really revolutionized the tutu.

Reprinted, by permission, from T. Bentley, *Costumes by Karinska*. www.tonibentley.com/pages/karinska_pages/karinska_excerpt3.html.

Even more to Madame Karinska's credit was her innovation of cutting the fabric on the bias for the bodices of all costumes. This meant that the fabric was cut on a diagonal instead of straight up and down. Using the fabric this way allowed for a certain amount of flexibility and stretch during performances. Dancers and opera singers are grateful for Barbara Karinska's contributions to the field of costume design.

► Madame Karinska created the powder puff tutu.

Take a Bow

The following two steps have you viewing, comparing, reflecting, and recording your work. These continue to be very important parts of assessing your work.

1. Look at a videotape of the dance piece without costumes and then in costume.

2. In your journal, record your observations of how the dance looked with and without costumes.

Did You Know? Isamu Noguchi and Martha Graham

Reprinted, by permission, from I. Noguchi, *The Isamu Noguchi garden museum.* Published with permission from the Isamu Noguchi Foundation, Inc., New York. www.noguchi.org.

There are times when choreographers see a prop or set and arrange a dance around that piece. A piece of sculpture can be the inspiration. One such famous set of collaborators was Martha Graham (1894-1991) and Isamu Noguchi (1904-1988). They collaborated for the first time in 1935 for a solo piece titled *Frontier.* Their collaboration lasted many years. One such collaboration was Graham's *Dance Seraphic Dialogue* (1955). You can find a list of dances for which Mr. Noguchi designed sets and props by searching the Internet with key words "Isamu Noguchi" and "Martha Graham." Many books about Isamu Noguchi and Martha Graham are also available. Peruse the bookstores—both online and in town—to find out more information about these two artists.

Herodiade, choreographed in 1944 by Ms. Graham with music by Paul Hindemith, is a prime example of props at work. Mr. Noguchi said, Within a woman's private world, and intimate space, I was asked to place a mirror, a chair, and a clothes rack. Salome dances before her mirror. What does she see? Her bones, the potential skeleton of her body. The chair is like an extension of her vertebrae; the clothes rack, the circumscribed bones on which is hung her skin. This is the desecration of beauty, the consciousness of time (www.noguchi.org/graham.html).

Lighting, Scenery, and Sound

₅,₆,₇,₈ Move It!

Scenery and lighting, like costumes and props, can influence and change choreography. Create a dance phrase. Go to a couple different sites, such as the cafeteria, a classroom, or bleachers in the gymnasium. Adapt the dance phrase to the new setting. This activity illustrates how a stage set can affect choreography.

Vocabulary

gel • strip lights • up full • venue • flat

Curtain Up

"Why do I have to know about the technical theater aspect of producing a dance piece?" is a question often asked. To get your wishes across to the crew (those people who make the lights, scenery, and sound work), who are working for and with you, you need a basic knowledge of the capabilities of your facility.

Lighting

Where you have your performance will dictate how much leeway and variation you can have with lights. Many schools do not have proper auditoriums or stages. Even if there is a stage it is often nothing more than a glorified speaker platform. If there is a stage space, you will usually find strip lights, which are lightbulbs (called lamps) mounted in a long, metal box with dividers for each one. They can be hung from the battens (poles) above the stage or set on the stage floor in the front. They are equipped with glass lenses that are alternately blue, red, and clear or white. The first rule of stage lighting is to make the performers visible. Mood and quality can come after, providing your space has the capacity for creativity. According to the budget of the dance or theater department, your teacher or adviser can recruit a lighting designer or technician from a local production company who can light your dance creatively. Again, you can offer your time as an intern to get such a company to look favorably at a reduced rate.

Many of today's schools use a cafetorium (which functions as a multipurpose room) as a performance space. The only lighting available is the regular ceiling fixtures. That means your only options are lights on or lights off. Think about renting or borrowing a follow spot or flood lights. Perhaps there is a regional theater in your area that is willing to share.

If you are fortunate enough to have a stage space, you may also have a light setup. Find and befriend the person in charge of the space; it may be a teacher, custodian, or audiovisual technician. Ask about what equipment is available for your use, who is allowed to work with that equipment, and if you can change the gels (the cellophane-like material that goes in front of the lighting instrument to produce colored light, creating the proper mood for your dance). You may have something very specific in mind, but you must maintain an open mind. Be realistic with your expectations. Ask others how they would accomplish the look you have in mind. If you are going to videotape a performance for a portfolio or local television broadcast, you must do it apart from a performance so that you can do it with the lights up to maximum capacity (or up full) (McGreevy-Nichols et al. 2001).

Scenery

For most novice choreographers scenery can get in the way. Learning to work with scenery is learning to account for the space it will occupy. Often rehearsals occur before you actually have the set constructed. This can be tricky. Many times you do not see or get to use scenery or set pieces until the week of the show. A simple strategy to use during rehearsals is to tape off the section of the floor on which the set will stand. When your plan is to dress the stage, you have to think in terms of help in designing, building, moving, and storing. There is also the matter of available money. One thing to consider is how long you want the scenery to last. Will there be a crew to move it on and off stage? Is there a place to build it and then store it? Is the stage large enough to accommodate the dancers as well as the scenery? Will a set piece do the job? Set pieces such as bushes, benches, mirrors, arches, and doorframes are very manageable and readily available, and they can be reused many times with a new paint job or trim.

Once your mind is set on the scenery, the next task is how to make it. You can start with four-by-eight-foot sheets of plywood or a frame covered with canvas. This is sometimes called a flat. You will need to think of ways to support the flats safely. Look to your school community and the community at large for help. Once you have the flat, you can paint your scene on it. Here again, your school community is a great resource. Flats also store easily against a wall and can be used multiple times.

If you only want a backdrop, and it will be in use for the entire performance, then brown industrial paper is the way to go. Put your scene on paper with paint; when it is dry, hang the paper on the back wall of the stage. This is called disposable scenery. For example, a show that is about the desert could have cacti and distant mountains painted on the paper. You are limited only by your imagination and by that of your helpers. Available money is also very important (McGreevy-Nichols et al. 2001).

Sound

What you need to know about sound is simple: Is there a sound system in the dance space? Do you need to provide sound equipment (CD or tape player), microphones, amplifiers, soundboard, and speakers? Does the owner of the performance space provide a technician who can set the sound levels and run the soundboard, or is that your responsibility? As with lighting instruments, you can always rent or borrow equipment to enhance your performance. You can do something as simple as putting a microphone in front of the speaker of the portable player that you use for class, but that means that the space needs to have some speakers somewhere.

Spotlight: Jennifer Tipton

Adapted from *Jennifer Tipton* (New York: American Ballet Theatre). www.abt.org/education/archive/designers/tipton_html. By permission of Jennifer Tipton.

Lighting designer Jennifer Tipton (1937-), renowned for her work in theater and dance lighting, was born in Columbus, Ohio, and attended Cornell University, where she studied English. After graduation, Ms. Tipton moved to New York to study dance. Her interest in lighting began with a course on the subject taught by Thomas Skelton at the American Dance Festival, Connecticut College. She has been awarded two Bessies and an Olivier for lighting dance. In 2003, she was given the first Jerome Robbins prize for her work in dance. Her work in that field includes pieces choreographed by Mikhail Baryshnikov, Trisha Brown, Jiri Kylian, Dana Reitz, Jerome Robbins, Paul Taylor, Twyla Tharp, and Dan Wagoner. Tipton has said that "99 and nine-tenths percent of the audience is not aware of the lighting, though 100 percent is affected by it" (www.news.cornell.edu/Chronicle/98/10.29.98/Tipton.html).

Take the Stage

In the case of planning the scenery, you must get used to the idea that you might have to make do with less if there are budget constraints. By using the following steps, you will have a workable plan.

1. As you read through the assignment, decide which of the dance phrases or dances you have created in previous chapters work best for this assignment.

2. Think about and then design (sketch) a set piece or stage set that befits the piece of choreography. (Remember that you want it to enhance the dance, not detract from it.) Think of it in two ways: You have a very limited budget, and you have no financial constraints.

3. Construct the set you designed for the limited budget. Find people to help you

with this task. You can't really expect to do this alone.

4. Use facsimiles (related copies of the designs) while you are working on the piece until the real set is ready.

5. Rehearse and refine choreography to work with the scenery. Don't wait until final dress rehearsal.

6. Make sure to videotape your dance and have photographs of the scenery to include in your portfolio (only if it is your design).

Take a Bow

Observing, reflecting, and recording are important to the assessment process. Follow these three steps:

1. Look at a videotape of the dance piece without scenery.

2. Study the designs, and imagine the dance in front of the design.

3. Record your impressions of how the dance looked without scenery as opposed to how you imagined it would look with it.

Did You Know? Fireproofing

There are many regulations concerning fireproofing scenery and set pieces. These regulations are set up by your local fire department. In recent years national news programs have reported incidents of fires that occurred because people didn't follow regulations; now there are stricter regulations in many areas of the country. In many venues (places where entertainment happens) where admission is charged, you may have to have a fire marshal in attendance. This trained fireman might do a flame test on curtains, drapes, and sometimes costumes. You can use materials and products to bring all of this up to code. Look under fireproofing companies and products in your local phone directory for more information.

Production Information and Time Line

5,6,7,8 Move It!

Gather your crew. You can have at least four but no more than six people. Together decide on how many measures (counts) you will use. Each member of the crew creates a dance phrase making special use of floor patterns. Give yourself a time limit. Perform your pieces all at once. The trick is to avoid being in anyone else's traffic pattern.

Vocabulary

mounting a production • theme-based • potpourri • strike • five Ws • cue to cue

Curtain Up

Mounting a production takes teamwork. When you hear the term *mounting a production* you can take it to mean putting together all the pieces that go into a show and getting it up on the stage. Following is a sample list of what needs to be done and who logically can do the jobs (this is notated in parentheses). The list can be shortened or taken into more detail as time and personnel allow. It can certainly be adapted to any project. Dividing the responsibility is sometimes difficult. You don't want anyone to think that they are being overworked. The point is that, even though you are a dancer, you should have a working knowledge of all of the jobs and tasks in order to have a production run smoothly. Sometimes a production is run entirely by students, but often you need the help of adults. They come in the form of advisers, community members, parents, and teachers. The following should be done in the order listed, unless otherwise noted.

- **At the very beginning of the project, when you are planning the production, and then again three weeks before the performance (students and adults).** Design (sketch) costumes, props, scenery, and lights. As you determine what you have for costumes and props, consider whether you need to adjust the choreography to accommodate these additions. The adjustments can be made to the choreography or the costume and prop design, and the changes happen by revision and reflection. Meet with technicians. The first meetings involve needs and wants. The later meetings will deal with what has actually been accomplished.

- **At the beginning of the project (adults). Choose dates, times, and place for the final performance.** The amount of stage space is important to many of the decisions you will make. Make sure that you and the people who usually use the space are clear

Production responsibilities

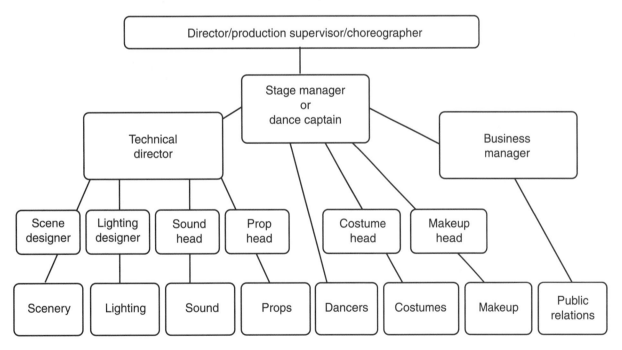

Audience

on the dates. Mark calendars and, where necessary, sign agreements.

- **At the beginning of the project (students).** Do research on the topics of the dances, list the ideas you wish to communicate, and decide whether you want the production to be theme-based (all the inspirations for the dances come from one major source or topic) or a potpourri of dances (each dance topic is independent of the others). You need to do this exercise to help you think about designing and crafting the costumes, props, scenery, and lighting.

- **Several weeks into the project (students; adviser; and people from industrial technology, theater, and home and consumer science classes).** Prioritize costume, props, lighting, scenery, and "extras" ideas that will affect and interact with the dances. Extras mean little additions that are not necessary but would make for a better, more embellished performance. Make lists of your needs. Consider what you can afford and how much time you have to devote to making these things happen. Find out who pays the technicians and whether the technicians are fellow students from a theater class.

- **In the weeks between the design and at least a week before the performance (students and adults). Construct costumes, props, scenery, and lighting plots.** There should be a meeting three weeks before the performance, when you will assess what has been accomplished and you can prioritize what is left to be done. It is also a time when you should begin to use the props, costumes, and set pieces. It is unreasonable to wait until final rehearsals to incorporate the use of props and set pieces. Be sure to secure enough backstage help for costume and scenery changes as well as a light board operator and a sound operator. All people involved—including performers—need to understand backstage behavior and etiquette.

- **Closer to the onset of the project, but can be adjusted throughout (students and adults).** If your concert is theme-based (all the dances are about one subject) or if you are presenting a story concert for a young audience, you should write a script and narration. This is not necessary for a potpourri concert (where none of the pieces relates to others in theme or style); but if the dances follow a theme, it is a nice addition.

- **A minimum of six weeks before the performance (students and adults).** Devise a publicity campaign. Most publicity campaigns fall short of success because there is a notion that publicity can happen at the last minute. The importance of publicity is to inform. List all the print media in your area. Write a press release of no more than one page, double-spaced. Be sure to include contact information. List local radio and TV stations, and send them a press release as well. Calling the stations ahead of time and asking how they like to receive information will make the job easier. Finally, create posters and widely distribute them.

- **Four to six weeks before the performance (students and adults).** Write and send press releases.

- **About a month before the performance (students and adults).** Put together the production like the final pieces of a puzzle. Collect materials for your souvenir program. This would include the order of the performance and names of the performers, the teachers involved in the project, the choreographers, all the people who helped (some with a special thank-you), and names of the technical crew. You will want a cover design with pertinent information such as time, date, location, title, and admission price (if applicable) on the cover. You might also want to include a written note or paragraph about the development of each piece. Revisions can be made on the computer up until the last week. Determine the amount of time you need for the programs to be ready for the performance. This will depend on whether you decide to use the services of a professional printing firm or whether your school can print the programs.

- **Three weeks before the performance (students and adults).** Send invitations and fliers. The letters of invitation and fliers should include where, when, what, why, and who, known as the five Ws.

- **About two weeks before the performance (students and adults).** Arrange for tickets and ticket sales. You can design a ticket on the computer. The ticket should include the name of the performance, the date and time of the performance, the place, the admission fee, and who is presenting. If there are performances on several different dates and times, and the public is invited, the date and time should be changed for each performance. You can sell tickets ahead of time, or you can limit sales to tickets at the door. You will need some very responsible people to take and sell tickets. Even if you do only door sales, it is important to have a ticket so that you can verify numbers of people against cash. Here is another place where you need and want help from people not performing. There should also be some accounting system set up. You and your teacher or adviser will want a record of tickets sold, total revenue, expenses, and who paid those fees. Recruit ushers. This is especially important if the seats are numbered.

- **Week of the performance.** Check with local media for the appropriate time frame for submitting information. Write and then call the newspapers. You might be able to get them to arrange an interview with students and teachers for a feature print article. Send faxes to the local TV stations. Send public service ads to the local media. Again, include the five Ws. A call to these people for their format, time frame, and deadlines is most helpful in getting them to air your message. This would be for them to cover the performance, not for advanced publicity.

- **About a week before the performance.** Write letters to parents and families inviting them to the performance. This letter should come from your teacher and would also have a permission slip attached if any of the performances were to take place in a time other than the school day or at a site other than your school.

- **Week of the performance (students and adults).** It is show time. You should schedule a technical rehearsal before the performers get on stage. This is when the light crew, scene crew, sound crew, costume crew, and prop crew refine what they have to do in order to make the show run. A stage manager has the final say on when the show goes up. Technical information sheets should be made for each dance, listing anything special that would concern the technical crew. They can then run a "cue to cue" rehearsal without the dancers. This means that the rehearsal involves running the music, sound, curtain, and light cues from the beginning of the show through the final curtain. Then the dancers should be added to the mix. Even if the performance space is not a stage but a gym, multipurpose room, or cafetorium, this technical rehearsal should take place. It makes the final dress rehearsal run much more efficiently.

  When you get to the dress rehearsal, don't panic. The performers will be excited. Don't expect everything to run smoothly. Remaining calm is of utmost importance. Getting things to run smoothly is why you have dress rehearsals. It is very difficult for you to be an integral part of the production crew during a performance if you are also performing.

- **Immediately after the show (students and adults).** Strike (take apart) the show by putting everything away. That means costumes, scenery, and props, all with hopes of recycling them. A postperformance team meeting is a good idea. This is where you can list the highs and lows of the project while it is still fresh in everyone's mind. Evaluation and taking note of what can be done better next time are important aspects of this meeting.

- **After performances are completed (students and adults).** Write and send thank-you notes to appropriate people. Make a folder of all the resources used and collected for the project (a project portfolio). This could include designs, construction records, light plots, programs, sample tickets, reviews, evaluation notes, names, and contacts for people who helped with the project as well as any financial information such as expenses and income.

Spotlight: Joseph Papp

Joseph Papp (1921-1991; born Papirofsky) was a producer. He was born in Brooklyn, New York.

From 1956 until his death, this daring producer was the founding director of The New York Shakespeare Festival. Starting with free performances in city parks, the company gradually became one of the most adventurous production companies in American theater, housing innovative productions of classics, new plays, and musicals. He opened the Public Theatre on Lafayette Street in 1967, where one of his first productions was the landmark rock musical *Hair* (1967). A musical adaptation of Shakespeare's *Two Gentlemen of Verona* (1971) went from a free run in Central Park to a Tony-winning success on Broadway.

He was not afraid to work with newcomers to the theatrical scene. Papp was open to all sorts of unusual projects. When choreographer Michael Bennett came to him with the idea of making a musical around the experiences of Broadway dancers, Papp gave the show a home. The result was *A Chorus Line* (1975), a massive hit that moved to Broadway, bringing the Public Theatre millions of dollars during its decade-plus run.

In the beginning run of the show the performers agreed to accept less than equity salary. No one had any idea what a hit the show would be. In turn they were to receive a percentage of the profits. The original cast members still reap the profits of that historic agreement. Papp, always innovative in what and how he produced, made great profits by mounting successful productions of works of dead authors, thereby eliminating the payment of rights.

Papp had some not-too-successful shows but always found a way to compensate for the losses. ". . . Papp was one of the most [prolific and] colorful theatrical personalities of his time." For more on what he produced, read *Joseph Papp: A Bio-Bibliography* (Horn 1992).

In the past, solo producers (Florenz Ziegfeld, David Merrick, Cheryl Crawford, etc.) had tremendous input into the creation of a show. Many important Broadway musicals began because such producers had an idea and then hired the composer and writers. Now, producers don't come into the process until a show is already written and tested. With production costs now in the tens of millions, it takes teams of a dozen or more producers to raise the funds for a show—making it impossible for any one of them to exercise creative control over a project.

Take the Stage

Teams function in more places than on athletic fields. A production team works together at the beginning of a project. The team members then go off and take care of their responsibilities. When they come back together, they put all the pieces of the production puzzle in place. When doing this work, be sure everyone takes and keeps notes (a journal).

1. Assemble a production team. This can be your dance classmates or others in the school community.

2. Assign, select, or recruit people for the jobs of costume designer and constructor, scenery or set piece designer or constructor, lighting designer and light board operator, and any other job you think needs to be done. Look at the lines of authority, who should answer to whom, in the responsibility chart.

3. Set this crew to the task of mounting the production of the dance pieces you have selected.

Take a Bow

For people not involved in theatrical productions of any kind, they do not have a clue as to the amount of work put in by all the individuals on the team. The following exercise documents the extent of the work. It is especially important that the people backstage get the recognition they so well deserve.

1. Collect all the notes that your production crew has taken from the start to the finish of the project.

2. Compile a portfolio of all the work with any comments from the crew written in appropriate places.

Did You Know? Stage Managers

Who is responsible for the whole production, from the beginning to the end? It is the stage manager. Stage managers coordinate productions from audition through rehearsal and performance periods. This is a huge job because this person is responsible for carrying out the wishes of the director or artistic director. The stage manager is the liaison between the performers, technical crew, and all the artistic staff. In the field of dance and musical theater there is a dance captain who is directly responsible for the dancers. Do a Web search with the key words "stage manager," or look at the June 2003 issue of *Dance Magazine* for more information.

CHAPTER 10

Review

Name _____ Class _____ Date _____

True/False

1. When you are videotaping a performance for portfolio or local television broadcast, you must do it apart from a performance so that you can do it with lights "up full." _____

2. Using props is an expensive way of dressing up your dances. _____

3. Only the crew need to understand backstage behavior and etiquette. _____

4. If the performance space is large, you do not need a technical rehearsal. _____

5. Fireproofing regulations are set by your local fire department. _____

6. A gel is the cellophane-like material that goes in front of the lighting instrument to produce colored light. _____

7. The stage manager has the ultimate responsibility once the show goes up. _____

Short Answers

1. What was one of Joseph Papp's biggest shows?

2. In the field of dance, who is comparable to the stage manager?

3. If you have a limited budget, where can you go for costumes?

4. Who took away the hoop aspect from the short tutu?

5. How can you keep scenery simple?

6. What does the term *mounting a production* mean?

7. Besides enhancing a dance, what can a costume do?

Who Does What?

Dancer

Choreographer

Stage manager

Dance captain

Producer

From *Experiencing Dance: From Student to Dance Artist* by H. Scheff, M. Sprague, and S. McGreevy-Nichols, 2005, Champaign, IL: Human Kinetics.

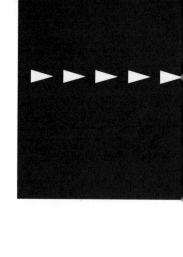

11

Learning to Dance in Different Ways: Your Training

▶▶▶▶▶▶▶▶▶▶▶▶▶▶▶▶▶▶

Lesson 11.1 Basic Techniques That Can Apply to All Dance Forms

Lesson 11.2 Different Schools of Dance Training

Lesson 11.3 Rehearsal and Performing Strategies

▶▶▶▶▶▶▶▶▶▶▶▶▶▶▶▶▶▶

From chapter 11 you will

1. learn that all dance forms use basic techniques that can be compared;
2. learn that every dance form has more than one technique behind it; and
3. learn how important it is to have good rehearsal and performance strategies and what they are.

Overture

ithin a single culture we find different dance
echniques, and styles. For instance, Japan
a rise in the frequency of where and when
appens. Of course, their traditional dance
assed down from generation to generation.
in traditional Japanese dance, about 120
st! In previous generations young children
osen to be trained in the traditional forms.
nt difficulty in passing on the tradition is
become expensive to take enough classes
e proficient.

has about two million people who do
dance at every possible opportunity they
njoyed by young and old. More recently
cing has become very popular with the
eople as they gather on the streets. It hit
ty in the 1970s but is still practiced by
dition to the traditional, ballroom, and
e styles, Japan has schools of Western
ance forms of ballet, modern, tap, and

Basic Techniques
That Can Apply
to All Dance Forms

5,6,7,8 Move It!

Perform a movement that contains three steps
(right, left, right). Perform it as a ballet pas de
bourrée (a three-step movement: step behind
you with the right foot, step to open with the
left foot, then step in front with the right); as a
modern dance triplet (basic waltz step: step forward in a plié with the right foot, step forward
in a relevé with the left foot, step forward in a
relevé with your right foot—"down, up, up");
as a popular dance, the pony; as a Latin mambo
or bachata (step side with right foot, step close
with left foot, step side with right foot and lift
left hip; and as a simple hula sideways step
(step, together, step). (If your teacher gives you
a rubric, make sure you refer to it as you work
on your dance combination.)

Vocabulary

Labanalysis • port des bras • pas de bourrée •
dance triplet • bachata • Laban efforts (weight,
time, space, and flow) • Laban effort actions
(punch, press, wring, slash, dab, flick, float,
and glide) • sissonne • allegro

Curtain Up

The instrument of dance is the body. Physics
and physiology remain constants. Hence, no
matter what dance form is being performed,
there are bound to be similarities in how the
body is used. Before a jump, or any other elevation, dancers bend their knees in preparation
for the takeoff and land with bent knees in
order to be ready for the next movement. The
spine flexes, extends, and rotates. Arms move
either in opposition to the torso and leg move-

ment or as complements to the movement in timing and direction. In dance, there are often specific, codified arm movements. Consider the ballet port des bras (carriage of the arms) or the symbolic arm movements in the hula. The dancer's focus generally helps the execution of the movement, as in spotting in turns. Eye movements can even be central to the dance form, as in Balinese and classical Indian dance. Feet move the dancers through space and keep time to the musical beat.

Many Western dance forms (such as ballet, jazz, Irish step, square, and contra dancing) use an upright alignment. Other forms may seem to address the earth with posture and focus (such as West African, Native American). Both types of alignment use the abdomen as an organizing place, and core (abdominal) strength is essential to efficient movement.

One way of observing and describing movement is called Labanalysis, which is a system created by Rudolf Laban and his followers. The system has descriptive definitions and vocabulary and is useful in improving movement. Labanalysis can be used to increase the range of motion, effectiveness, and expressive ability. Effort is the attitude toward the energy that is exerted when doing a movement. "It is 'how' a movement is performed or the 'quality' of the movement. By 'attitude' we mean your inner feeling toward the movement while performing it. For example, you can walk slowly as if it is a lazy summer day or you can walk slowly as if you are fearful that you are in danger" (McGreevy-Nichols et al. 2001, p. 17).

Effort has four elements: weight, time, space, and flow. Attitude toward weight can be strong (expending much energy) or light (using a fine or delicate touch). A punch uses strong weight, and a dab uses light weight. Attitude toward time can be sudden (showing urgency or anxiety) or sustained (showing a relaxed, easygoing feeling). A flick uses sudden time, and a pressing action uses sustained time. Attitude toward space may be direct (the movement has a single focus) or indirect (the movement has many foci). Gliding uses direct space, and floating uses indirect space. Attitude toward flow can be bound (controlled) or free (uncontrolled). A wringing action uses bound flow, and a slash uses free flow. Combinations of three of the effort elements (weight, time, and space) are called basic effort actions. These actions are punch (strong weight, sudden time, and direct space), float (light weight, sustained time, and indirect space), glide (light weight, sustained time, and direct space), slash (strong weight, sudden time, and indirect space), dab (light weight, sudden time, and direct space), wring (strong weight, sustained time, and indirect space), flick (light weight, sudden time, and indirect space), and press (strong weight, sustained time, and direct space) (McGreevy-Nichols et al. 2001).

Use the terms you just read about to improve your execution of familiar dance steps as well as unfamiliar steps. If you know a sissonne (an elevation from two feet and landing on one foot) is to be executed with direct space, light weight, and sudden time, then you have a pretty good idea that you are doing an allegro (fast, quick-footed) movement. Analyze a movement that is strange to you according to these Laban efforts, then try to add the correct efforts to the movements of the body parts. With this strategy, your execution of the new movement should be clearer.

 Take the Stage

Whether you prefer one dance form over another, it is important for you to be able to discern similarities in approach and technique among different genres. This knowledge will help you see how you can use your body in similar ways no matter which genre you are using, such as ballet, modern, lyrical, jazz, or world dance.

Chose four different dance forms. Take a class in each or watch a video of each type in order to determine how the body is used in each dance form.

Take a Bow

Note any similarities among the dance forms you chose in Take the Stage. Fill out the Technique and Style Comparison Chart on page 153.

Spotlight: Erick Hawkins

Adapted from www.americandancefestival.org/Archives/scripps/hawkins.html).

Erick Hawkins (1909-1994) discovered dance while studying at Harvard. He was the first student to enroll in George Balanchine's School of American Ballet in 1934. In 1938, he was the first male dancer to join the Martha Graham Dance Company functioning as both a dancer and choreographer, where he stayed until 1950. In 1951, Hawkins opened his own school. It was at this time that he became interested in the new field of kinesiology, learning as much as possible about how the body moves and how to avoid injuring it. He began to develop a modern dance technique that was fluid and graceful and continues to influence dancers throughout the world. You can learn more about the technique of Erick Hawkins by reading *The Erick Hawkins Modern Dance Technique* by Renata Celichowska, available at major online bookstores, or you can watch the technique performed in the following videos: *Erick Hawkins' America*, *The Erick Hawkins Modern Dance Technique Volume I: Principles and Floor Warm-Up,* and *The Erick Hawkins Modern Dance Technique Volume II: Movement Patterns and Aesthetic Principles.*

Did You Know? Authentic Movement

Authentic movement is a form of dance, body, and movement therapy. It has different definitions, one from the East Coast, one from the West Coast, and many variations within those definitions. It is used to construct healthy movement patterns. It links the conscious and the unconscious with movement and no words.

Different Schools of Dance Training

5,6,7,8 Move It!

Take a combination that you learned in a class and change it to fit your personal style (how you would like to do the combination).

Take a Bow:
Dance Form Technique and Style Comparison Chart

Name _____ Class _____ Date _____

Did you take a class or watch a video? _____

Instructions: Put a check mark next to the items that are used by the dance form technique and style.

Laban efforts

Space: [ ] direct   [ ] indirect

Time: [ ] sudden   [ ] sustained

Flow: [ ] bound   [ ] free

Weight: [ ] strength   [ ] lightness

Special body, leg, or arm positions:
    Alignment

Description of body use:
    Arms

    Legs

    Knees

    Spine (torso)

    Focus

Use of space:
    Near space

    Far space

    Formations (set or random)

    Relationships between dancers (partners, groups, small kinesphere, large kinesphere):

Special clothing or accessories:

Vocabulary

Cecchetti • Balanchine • Royal Academy of Dance (RAD) • Bournonville • Russian Vaganova • petit allegro • Ruth St. Denis •

Isadora Duncan • Martha Graham • Doris Humphrey • Charles Weidman • Lester Horton • Matt Mattox • Luigi • Bob Fosse

Curtain Up

The following information is adapted from www.the-ballet.com/techniques.php.

The dance forms of ballet, modern, and jazz all have variations of the same basic techniques. For the most part these techniques were developed by and named for the people who perfected them. In ballet the major methods are Cecchetti, Russian Vaganova, Royal Academy of Dance (RAD), Bournonville, and Balanchine. The Cecchetti technique was developed from the teachings of the ballet master Enrico Cecchetti (and protected and taught to prospective teachers) by the Cecchetti Society. The Russian Vaganova technique is named after and derived from the teachings of Agrippina Vaganova, who was the artistic director of the Kirov Ballet. The Royal Academy of Dance syllabus was started in England. It has a very specific ballet syllabus with grading levels. Students at each level wear a different color so that people watching can discern the level of the student. Dancers also learn and perfect specific dances. Now the RAD syllabus is taught all over the world along with the other techniques mentioned. The American School of Ballet teaches the Balanchine method, which is named after its creator, George Balanchine. He modified the Vaganova method to enable his dancers to use rapid footwork (petit allegro). Agrippina Vaganova studied under August Bournonville in the 1890s. When you go to a ballet school in your community, you might encounter just one of the styles mentioned here; however, many ballet instructors now teach a combination of all these techniques.

In modern dance, pioneers Ruth St. Denis and Isadora Duncan paved the way for the next generation of modern dancers to develop the techniques and styles used in this dance form. Three notable techniques in this form were developed by Martha Graham, Doris Humphrey, Charles Weidman, and Lester Horton. Graham's technique is based on the principles of contraction and release. The Humphrey-Weidman technique is based on the principles of suspension, fall, and recovery. Horton's technique uses a strong center (torso) and asymmetrical arm and leg movements. These techniques and styles are so well documented that they are still being taught today. You can learn more about these techniques and styles through videos, books, and participation in dance classes. Now many modern dance choreographers think it is important for dancers who perform with them to take their classes so that they learn the choreographers' styles.

In jazz dance, you can study the techniques of Matt Mattox, Luigi, and Bob Fosse, among others. Mattox's exercises help the dancer isolate movement of body parts. The Mattox movement style comes from the Jack Cole style, modern, ethnic, flamenco, tap dance, and his own studies in ballet. It is based on his belief that all forms of dance are valid as inspiration and expression. Mattox (1921-) has commented on his need for total freedom in expression by calling his style "freestyle" (Frich 1983). Eugene Louis Facciuto (1925-), more commonly known as Luigi, was an experienced, trained dancer who suffered a near-fatal car accident that left him paralyzed on his right side. This led him to develop a series of dance exercises as rehabilitation. They became the basis for his style. The first principle is to use an imaginary barre to help stabilize the body (isometrics). The second principle is feeling from inside: "Watch it, feel it and then move" (Kreigel, Person, and Roach 1997, p. 6). Bob Fosse (1927-1987) created a style that is recognizable in all his work throughout four decades on Broadway. The overall look of the technique displays a rounded shoulder, hip popping, elbow jutting, splayed hand, and finger snapping, with the signature use of a derby. Classes are readily available in all these techniques.

► The famous Fosse pose.

Take the Stage

Whether you are more comfortable with ballet, jazz, modern, or another dance form, you can create a dance phrase or combination and vary it by using two different styles.

1. Choose a dance form that uses multiple techniques and styles.
2. Analyze the differences between the individual techniques and styles within the same dance form using the information from lesson 11.2 Curtain Up and your own research and the lessons 11.1 and 11.2 Technique and Style Comparison Chart on page 153.
3. Create a dance phrase. Perform it sequentially in two different styles in the same dance form.

Take a Bow

Present the dance phrase in both styles. Have your peers use the dance form comparison chart on page 153 to analyze the differences between the two styles.

Spotlight: C.K. Ladzekpo

Reprinted, by permission, from C.K. Ladzekpo, www.bmrc.berkeley.edu/people/ladzekpo.Bio.html.

World dance forms have their masters just as Western dance forms do:

C.K. Ladzekpo (1944-) is the director of the African music program at the University of California at Berkeley. He has combined a brilliant career as a performer, choreographer, and composer with teaching and extensive scholarly research into African performing arts. He is a member of a famous family of African musicians and dancers who traditionally serve as lead drummers and composers among the Anlo-Ewe people of southeastern Ghana in West Africa. C.K. Ladzekpo has been a lead drummer and instructor with the Ghana National Dance Ensemble, the University of Ghana's Institute of African Studies, and the Arts Council of Ghana. He joined the music faculty of the University of California at Berkeley in 1973 and remains an influential catalyst of the African perspective in the performing arts. In 1973 he founded the critically acclaimed African Music and Dance Ensemble. As the company's artistic director, choreographer, and master drummer, he has led in many pioneering African dance and polyrhythmic percussion ensemble music presentations at major venues in the United States, Canada, and Europe. He has been artistic director of the Mandeleo Institute in Oakland since 1986. C.K. Ladzekpo's modern concert stage rendition of *Atsiagbeko*, a traditional war dance drumming suite of the Anlo-Ewe, is one of the features in the television documentary 'African Dance at Jacob's Pillow Dance Festival' which continues to be a popular broadcast since its national premiere in 1988 on PBS.

Did You Know? African Drums

The following information comes from www.cnmat.berkeley.edu/~ladzekpo/Foundation.html.

Among the Anlo-Ewe, a legendary metaphor, "'ela kuku dea 'gbe wu la 'gbagbe," which means, "a dead animal cries louder than a live one," is commonly used to explain the human experience that inspired the origin of the drum. So when the need came to communicate louder, a super voice surrogate was built out of a skin of a dead animal that could deliver the message louder and clearer.

Drum making is an ancient art. Drumming and dance are inseparable. The process starts with the selection of an appropriate log. Some drum makers believe that there is a merging of three spirits when making a drum: the log or tree spirit, animal spirit from the skin, and the energy of the carver. After the log is carved animal skins are prepared, cured, and stretched over the circumference. The metal rings and ropes not only hold the skins in place but also give each drum an individual voice and tone (www.eartheart.co.za/drums.htm).

► Drummers in action.

© Bruce Davis

► Lesson 11.3

Rehearsal and Performing Strategies

5,6,7,8 Move It!

With a partner, select a section of a dance you have learned. Each of you practice separately, perform it for each other, and then perform it together in front of a mirror.

Vocabulary

critique • sweat equity • dance coach •

triple threat

Curtain Up

In the professional world, dancers are valued not only for their technical abilities but also for their malleability or adaptability. Choreographers and dance directors expect their dancers to work hard and act on corrections and critiques immediately. Dancers are expected to be good team players, helpful and patient with other dancers as well as active participants in the process. (Some choreographers rely heavily on dancer-created movement, whereas others expect only execution of their steps and movement. Dancers should be sensitive to which role is expected of them.)

The following are some rehearsal strategies:

- Write the dance down and then use these notes to practice your dance correctly.
- Practice your steps with someone else.
- Have someone watch you and give you a critique (corrections).
- Work on the parts that you have the most trouble with.
- Create a rhythmic chant pattern to help you remember a difficult part ("When I do the box step, my hands go back").

- Try to perform the dance without anyone's help.
- Use sweat equity—in other words, work hard.
- Memorize the words, music, counts, and visual cues as necessary to the performance of the dance.

The following are some performance strategies:

- Always warm up.
- Review problem spots in your dances.
- Concentrate. Do your work.
- Find some quiet time to help you remain calm and focused.
- Be quiet in and around the performing area.
- Before your entrances, get into character (the correct quality of movement).
- If you make a mistake, continue on as if nothing has happened.
- When exiting, continue performing until you are well past the wings and exit area.

The following are some rehearsal and performance strategies for solos:

- Work on phrasing and clarity of execution.

- Express the emotional content of the dance work.
- Make changes in how you do the movement that make sense for you. A solo should make sense to your body.
- Use your personal style and unique characteristics of your dancing.
- During the rehearsal process, communicate your needs and opinions to the choreographer. Incorporate into your work the critiques from the choreographer and rehearsal director.

The following are some rehearsal and performance strategies for ensemble dances:

- Counts and movements need to be unified and exact.
- During unison sections, both impulses and breath rhythms among the dancers need to be together.
- Focus and facial expressions are the same.
- Angles of facings are set.
- Leg and arm movements, even the height of the leg, are coordinated among all the dancers.

 Take the Stage

You can be the best judge of what helps you improve your work. The following exercise will help.

1. Using a dance or section of a dance you are currently working on, apply the rehearsal strategies and behaviors from the previous lists.

2. Use the information on performing as you approach your next performance.

 Take a Bow

Learning about the strategies is one thing, but putting them into practice is another. You will want a record of what strategies worked best for you and why. (If your teacher gives you a rubric, make sure you refer to it as you work on your dance composition or study.)

1. In your journal, evaluate how the rehearsal and performance strategies and behaviors affected your performance.

2. Have members of the audience, your teacher, and your peers evaluate your rehearsal and performance by using the rehearsal and performance evaluations (supplied by your teacher).

Spotlight: Fred Astaire

Quotes from www.fredastaire.net/biography/rko.htm: adapted from Billman 1997.

Fred Astaire's (1899-1987) career spanned decades and covered many venues. He had a lasting impact on cinema, dance, stage, television, and music. Besides being multitalented (he sang, danced, and acted, which is called a *triple threat*), he was a strong negotiator at contract time. He came to his film career already a star. Astaire was granted his request of five to six weeks of rehearsal before filming began. "He and Hermes Pan began creating dance numbers that came out of the plot and were conceived with the camera in mind. Rather than using tricks or complicated edits, Astaire insisted that the camera catch him and [Ginger] Rogers in full figure in extended shots, allowing the audience to see the entire dance sequence."

Did You Know? Dance Coach

A dance coach is a person who passes on a specific piece of choreography to another dancer as accurately as possible. Many times this person was an original dancer in the piece, as was the case of Judith Jamison (1943-), who passed on the piece *Cry* to other dancers in Alvin Ailey's dance company. Mr. Ailey created this piece for Ms. Jamison in 1971. Other coaches include Ann Reinking (1949-), who has passed on the dances and style of Bob Fosse. Alexandra Danilova (1903-1997), for whom George Balanchine ultimately created 18 ballets, became a coach for his works. Although she gave her last performance in 1957 at the age of 54, she continued to share her vast knowledge of the classical repertoire with many other dancers. You can see Madame Danilova in the film *The Turning Point* (1977), where she actually coaches a young dancer for a role.

© 2003. Steward Photography

▶ Dance coaches fine tune their dancers.

CHAPTER 11

Review

Name _____ Class _____ Date _____

Fill in the Blank

1. No matter what dance form is being performed, there are bound to be (differences, similarities) in how the body is used.

2. Western European dance forms and West African dance forms both depend on (vertical alignment, core strength) as the basis for movement.

3. Adagio is the tempo opposite from allegro. Circle all the words that would describe the term adagio: fast, slow, controlled, sudden, sustained, free.

4. All the early modern dancers based their techniques on (the same, different) principles.

5. Traditional African drum making (does, does not) include a spiritual aspect.

6. A kick uses (light, strong) weight, (sustained, sudden) time, and (indirect, direct) space.

Short Answers

1. What are the differences between performance strategies for solos and performance strategies for ensembles?

2. What are the two different ways choreographers work with dancers?

3. Describe the three different jazz styles listed in lesson 11.2 Curtain Up.

4. Give examples (other than those in the text) of the following Laban terms: strong weight, light weight, sudden time, sustained time, direct space, indirect space, free flow, and bound flow.

Essay

What are the similarities and differences among the four different dance forms that you researched in lesson 11.1? Analyze and explain why you have a preference for one form over the others.

 From *Experiencing Dance: From Student to Dance Artist* by H. Scheff, M. Sprague, and S. McGreevy-Nichols, 2005, Champaign, IL: Human Kinetics.

Dealing With Realities: Actions That Can Help You Become a Better Performer

▶▶▶▶▶▶▶▶▶▶▶▶▶▶▶▶▶▶▶▶▶▶▶▶   ▶▶▶▶▶▶▶▶▶▶▶▶▶▶▶▶

▶▶▶▶▶▶▶▶▶▶▶▶▶▶▶▶

From chapter 12 you will

1. locate resources within your community that can help you expand your dance technique and training;

2. describe and prepare a lecture and demonstration on a dance form; and

3. understand the importance of knowing how to practice correctly.

Overture

"I think the best thing to do in seeking a good teacher is to ask the advice of a well-known professional, an experienced dancer. If you admire a dancer, find out where she studied" (Balanchine 1954, p. 57).

How many times have you seen performers and wondered how they got to be so good at what they do? Who taught them so well that they can outperform others? How much is the result of raw talent, and how much do they owe to the honing of their skills by a good teacher? The short answer to these questions is that these performers were able to learn and apply what talented and giving teachers had to offer.

You Deserve the Best

5,6,7,8 Move It!

Take a master class or a class from a different teacher. Master class teachers are ranked at the top of their field; therefore, they have earned the title of master. Write down two or three important or new pieces of information you learned from that teacher, and then share this information with classmates.

 Vocabulary

dance company school • apprentice • master class • dance class etiquette

 Curtain Up

How do you find the best kind of dance training to fulfill your needs? You must decide what is important for you. Even if you don't plan to go into a more rigorous study of dance, you can become an educated consumer, both as a student and as one who goes to performances. In most areas of the world there aren't any government regulations or licensing of schools of dance. Sometimes dance teachers simply grow up taking classes in one or two places and work as apprentices for their teachers. Apprentices work with mentors and learn directly from them. Once apprentices complete their training, they then open their own studios and give their students the same experience they had. Sometimes this experience is good, but sometimes the experience falls short of what it could be.

You need to find what is best for you. You can look to your community to find resources:

- You can take master classes and workshops given by presenters in a particular dance form. These may occur when a college or university brings in a guest artist and opens the class to the community.

Photo courtesy of Ben Scheff.

► Character dance class adds to your experience as a dancer.

- You could take dance classes from several different people in the community. This will expose you to a variety of teaching styles and dance techniques.
- Sometimes apprenticeships are offered with junior dance companies and organizations with cultural ties (i.e., Bolivian, Korean, Thai, Cambodian, Russian). Apprenticeships give you the opportunity to work with an existing group. The experience also can expose you to careers related to dance.
- A dance company school is a good place to observe and take a class. These schools are usually affiliated with a professional dance company.
- You can make special arrangements to take or observe classes with conservatories, colleges, and universities. They sometimes open classes to the public. You can also ask if you can audit the class, which means that you attend the class but do not receive credit.

In your search for the most ideal place for your dance training, here are some things to keep in mind:

- Take your time.
- Visit many places that teach the dance forms that interest you.

- See what credentials the teachers have.
- Check whether their students have gone on to do well in the field of dance and dance-related areas.
- Speak with the students of the school about their experiences both in class and outside of class.
- You may live in an area with only a few choices, which means you may have to consider traveling to a place that is not as convenient for your family.

You should be able to make good judgments based on what you have learned in dance at school. Following are some things to look for:

1. Is the instructor certified in some way by a national or international organization? Ask about professional credentials.
2. Is there a planned syllabus? Each class should include a proper warm-up, and the material presented should follow from simple to more complex.
3. Does the instructor take part in or belong to a dance service organization?
4. Does the instructor take advantage of continuing education opportunities such as seminars and workshops conducted by leading dance educators?
5. Is the accompanying music appropriate for the dance form?
6. Is the facility clean and well ventilated? Is the floor smooth and safe?
7. Are the class sizes appropriate to the space and dance form? There should be enough students to make it a class, but not so many so that your movement is restricted.
8. Because performing is part of a well-rounded dance education, are such opportunities available in this school?
9. Does the instructor take time to explain corrections?
10. Do the students look as though they are having a good time while training?
11. Is the atmosphere friendly and nurturing?

12. Does the instructor teach and demonstrate good technique (proper alignment, correct positions, correct terminology)? You can ask about the rate of injuries to this teacher's students.

13. Did the students use proper dance class etiquette? (There should be very limited conversation among the students. The focus is on the teacher and corrections. There should be proper use of personal space.)

14. Was the program recommended by more than a few people or by someone you trust?

 Take the Stage

Now you want to expand on your dance education. Where do you go? What should you do? Following these steps will give you a frame of reference:

1. Research your community for places where dance instruction occurs. Choose schools that offer classes in your field of interest (ballet, tap, jazz, modern, ethnic, world). Visit two schools, watch some classes, and observe what is being taught and how it is taught.

2. Watch for students' reactions to the instructor and to the other students.

3. Plan an interview with the instructors. You may have to do this at a separate time.

4. Write down your observations of the teachers. (Refer to the checklist on page 165.) Make at least three points. Describe the basic technique taught.

5. Write your observation of the students. (Refer to the checklist on page 165.)

6. Compare and contrast findings between the two schools.

 Take a Bow

What can you do with the information that you and your peers have collected from the exercise in Take the Stage? You can provide a service for fellow dancers by doing the following activity.

1. Compile a list of dance schools (including their contact information) and programming available to you. Include the forms of dance they teach.

2. Assemble the class' research to make a training resources guide.

 Spotlight: New York City High School of Performing Arts

The school that is portrayed in the movie *Fame* is the legendary High School of Performing Arts, now known as LaGuardia School of the Arts. The building that housed the school was on West 46th Street in New York City. When the High School of Performing Arts combined with the High School of Music and Art, the school moved to a new building next door to Lincoln Center. The original concept for the school was that students who were interested in the performing arts should have a public school where they could receive professional training. Many of the students have gone on to professional careers in dance, drama, and music. Whether they are still actually performing, teaching, managing, or enjoying their art form, their experiences as academic students with half a day in "shop" classes has had a tremendous impact on their lives. This school was the model for many public and private schools of the arts that now exist across the country.

Take the Stage: Checklist for Observation and Interview for Dance Training Facility

Check off the items that you observed.

Instructor

____ Is the instructor certified by some national or international organization? Ask about professional credentials.

____ Does the instructor take part in or belong to a dance service organization?

____ Does the instructor take advantage of continuing education opportunities such as seminars and workshops conducted by leading dance educators?

____ Since performing is part of a well-rounded dance education, does the instructor make such opportunities available?

Class and Environment

____ Is there a planned syllabus? Each class should include a proper warm-up, and the material presented should follow from simple to more complex.

____ Is the accompanying music appropriate for the dance form?

____ Is the facility clean and well ventilated? Is the floor smooth and safe?

____ Are the class sizes appropriate to the space and dance form? There should be enough students to make it a class, but not so many so that your movement is restricted.

____ Does the instructor take time to explain corrections?

____ Do the students look as though they are having a good time while training?

____ Is the atmosphere friendly and nurturing?

____ Does the instructor teach and demonstrate good technique (proper alignment, correct positions, correct terminology)? You can ask about the rate of injuries to this teacher's students.

____ Did the students use proper dance class etiquette? (There should be very limited conversation among the students. The focus is on the teacher and corrections. There should be proper use of personal space.)

____ Was the program recommended by more than a few people or by someone you trust?

Did You Know? Professional Dance Education Organizations

Many national, regional, and local professional organizations provide services and support to dancers and dance educators. These organizations are resources about the field of dance education and serve different sectors (studios, public schools, higher education, performers, companies, researchers, and so on). Many professional organizations offer workshops, conferences, resource lists and links, advocacy help, and Internet bulletin boards with news and announcements along with other services. Here are four such national organizations: National Dance Education Organization, Dance Masters of America, Dance Educators of America, and National Dance Association. Be sure to check out their Web sites.

Presenting a Lecture/Demonstration on a Dance Form

5,6,7,8 **Move It!**

Do you remember the game "show and tell" in elementary school? Select a simple dance exercise. Demonstrate it (show). Explain not only how to do the exercise but also its benefits (tell). Your goal is for people to get a better understanding of the dance.

Vocabulary

lecture/demonstration

Curtain Up

A lec/dem (lecture/demonstration) is a presentation that combines a lecture on a specific topic with a demonstration that highlights the main points of the information. This lecture is enriched by a miniperformance that augments what is being presented. The text for the lecture can be interspersed with the demonstration. In the case of dance, the demonstration often illuminates the points of the lecture about a specific dance form or style. A lecture/demonstration can be very helpful to people who want an understanding of a specific dance form but don't have the time or inclination to enter into a long-term study of that form.

Dance companies use lecture/demonstrations or audience building and educational and community outreach. School dance programs use them for advocacy, telling what they do in the program and what students learn through the program. Another way to use lec/dems is as service to the community, bringing dance as an art form and as an instructional tool to people who would ordinarily not be exposed to the benefits of dance education. Students can use the format for demonstrating their knowledge of dance, or they can use dance for demonstrating knowledge of other subject areas.

Since there are so many learning styles, and different people learn differently, a lecture/demonstration is a perfect tool for getting a message across. People who learn by listening get the verbal message, and people who learn by seeing get the visual message.

Take the Stage

What kind of procedure can you use to put together a lecture/demonstration? The following steps will be a big help.

1. Select the dance form you will use. You may want to do additional research to make a better presentation.

2. Select two or three important points to talk about when preparing your lecture on the dance form or style you are presenting. You can use note cards to help you remember the points you want to make.

3. Create a combination that includes and demonstrates the points you talked about in your lecture.

4. Rehearse your lecture/demonstration. In an informal setting present the information and teach the combination you created to your classmates.

► World dance with traditional apparel helps your audience understand dances from other cultures.

Take a Bow

1. Have your lecture/demonstration video-taped. Videotape the other lec/dems done by your classmates.

2. Compare and contrast what you presented with a similar style presented by other classmates.

3. Compare the content and delivery of the lec/dem.

4. Create a two-column chart with one column listing the likenesses and one column listing the differences.

Spotlight: Donald McKayle

Dancer, director, choreographer, and educator Donald McKayle (1930-) has done it all since beginning his career in 1948. McKayle is known for choreographing such classic works as *Games, Rainbow 'Round My Shoulder, District Storyville,* and *Songs of the Disinherited.* Many well-known people in the field have been members of McKayle's company, including Elliot Feld, Arthur Mitchell, Lar Lubovitch, Gus Solomon Jr., and Alvin Ailey.

Knowing the importance of passing on his knowledge, McKayle, a full professor of dance at the University of California at Irvine, has served on the faculties of many prominent institutions. He has also created an etude for the American Dance Legacy Institute based on *Rainbow 'Round My Shoulder.* For more information on this project and Donald McKayle, do a Web search with key words "American Dance Legacy Institute" and "Donald McKayle."

Did You Know? Different Ways to Learn

There has been some controversy with taking traditional world dance forms, such as Native American and African dance, and presenting them within a formal dance performance setting. Because many ethnic dance forms are used within a culture's rituals and religion, members of those cultures are often concerned that their cultural dance is being commercialized when presented on the stage. One way to avoid this kind of controversy is to introduce ethnic forms through lecture/demonstrations. This way you can educate the audience and honor the culture while showing the dance. For instance, African dance uses call and response as a structure for their dances. Usually the drummers lead the dancers through the dance with a certain rhythm signaling the change of step. Be sure to incorporate the traditional structure of the dance such as call and response in African dance. Also be sure to thoroughly research the cultural form you plan to present, being careful to use the older traditional style as opposed to the more popularized versions that may evolve within a cultural form.

Practice Makes Permanent

5,6,7,8 Move It!

Review a dance or dance phrase that you have recently learned. Close your eyes and try to see it in your mind's eye.

Vocabulary

practice • rehearsal • downtime • neuron •   kinesthetic • imagery • self-concept

Curtain Up

Practice does not always make perfect, but it does make permanent. "Practice refers to learners repeating a skill over time" (Sousa 2001, p. 97). Performing artists call this practice *rehearsal*. First one learns and rehearses the new skills. Another rehearsal should occur after a downtime of about six hours (the time it takes to set the new learning by organizing and coordinating the movements and their timing within the brain). This rehearsal will assign more neurons (nerve cells in the brain) to work with the skill, which increases the skill's efficiency and clarity of performance. These neurons will be connected to the skill for as long as the skill is used, hence the saying "Use it or lose it." Have you ever felt "rusty" returning to class after a long vacation? Perhaps the brain may need some extra time to recall the particular kinesthetic (movement skill) after not using the skill for a while.

Although David Sousa says, "Practice makes permanent," he also quotes Vince Lombardi, the famous football coach, as saying, "Perfect practice makes perfect." Before you spend hours honing a new dance skill or rehearsing a new piece of choreography, make sure that your own understanding of the movement is correct. The person who taught you the movement should have presented the skill in learnable sections and demonstrated it correctly and clearly. The teacher or choreographer should have watched you perform the movement or dance and corrected any missteps or misinterpretations. Only then can you effectively practice on your own.

Another helpful learning strategy for movement and dances is to go over the new learning in your mind just before falling asleep. Storage of information in the brain occurs during the deep sleep periods. This is when the day's events and learning are sorted and stored in the brain. Taking yourself through a mental practice (imagery) just before sleeping helps link the new learning with previous experiences that ensure memory.

To make sure you truly learn the material, it should hold meaning for you. The new learning has to make sense, and perhaps there is also some emotional connection for you. The process of making meaning out of new information sends it to the long-term memory. Without emotional or meaningful connections, the brain will not store information, including the kinesthetic information. How many times have you improvised incredible movement and then just a short time later haven't been able to recall it? It was lost forever and you had to settle for another constructed movement. The brain wasn't forced to pay attention to this movement through an emotional reaction, or it wasn't linked to a past experience for meaning. The perfect movement was lost forever.

Did you know that one can actually practice a skill without getting better? To improve the performance of a skill, the learner must do the following (Hunter 1982):

- Has to want to improve
- Has to have enough knowledge to figure out the different ways the skills can be applied
- Has to understand how to apply the knowledge to a situation
- Can evaluate the performance and decide what should be changed to improve performance.

Self-concept, or the way we view ourselves, may also affect the process of rehearsal. If there has been a similar successful experience in the past, a positive self-concept will allow the learner to feel confident. Self-confidence makes for good learners. If there is a negative self-concept, caused by a past unsuccessful experience, the learner will be uncertain and reluctant to engage in the work. Are you usually eager to tackle a challenge, or are you reluctant as you approach a task? Try to approach a rehearsal while in a positive and confident state of mind. This will ensure a productive practice session.

Poor or inadequate training and practice can lead to injury and dead ends in technical improvement. Retraining is a long and difficult process. You can't just plow through a block in your technical improvement. You must unlearn and correctly relearn a skill once it is practiced. In a sense, the brain and body must be rewired. You're required to change muscle memory, and you have to lay new neural pathways. To correct the performance of the learned skill, you must be very motivated to change. You need to undergo honest evaluation of the problem and use a patient, informed retraining strategy. Maintain constant awareness of the retraining focus throughout the practice or rehearsal. For instance, if you are practicing abdominal support for alignment, you need to be constantly aware of abdominal use throughout the day as well as during dance class.

If practice is to make permanent, then you must pay careful attention to how it is structured and carried out. Good luck with your perfect practice so that you can make your learning perfect!

 Take the Stage

It is frustrating to continually have the same problem with a step or skill or position. It can also be difficult to see what is causing the problem. The following exercise can help:

1. Take a physical problem that you may be having in a technique class.

2. Have a conference with your teacher about the possible reasons for the problem.

3. Get a second opinion and compare and contrast opinions. This might be from a physical therapist or a dance medicine professional or some of your other teachers.

 Take a Bow

Devise a plan for overcoming the technical problem with small, achievable goals.

After working through your plan, analyze how your plan for overcoming the technique problem worked. For example, if your problem was a pirouette, try working through the following information (this works for all dance forms):

1. Stand in first position.
2. Tendu your right leg to the side. At the same time, open your arms to the side (à

la seconde, or second position).

3. Slide (tendu) your right foot on the floor behind you in fourth position. At the same time, your right arm comes in front of you as if you are holding a beach ball. You are in demi-plié.

4. Advance the right arm to the side. This is one of the ways we learned to pirouette— it levels your shoulders in advance of the actual turn. Push the left arm to meet the right arm while rising up on demi-pointe on the left leg and raising the right foot

to the left knee. Complete a quarter turn. Hold the position in relevé with perfect alignment.

5. Lower the right leg, open the arms, and remain in demi-plié.

6. Repeat this in quarters, completing the circle. Then do half turns and full turns using the same technique. Reverse and do these to the left.

7. Videotape your multiple turns before you practice the exercise, and then after. Compare the two.

You will find that when done properly, this exercise will enable you to improve your turning abilities.

Spotlight: Lynn Simonson

Lynn Simonson (1943-) has been teaching the Simonson Technique, as it has come to be known, for more than 30 years and has trained teachers in 15 countries. The technique has four basic principles: that dancers can dance injury-free throughout [their] lifetime; that every student can be taught to dance; that the whole of the person is recognized; and that the rhythms, energy and styles of jazz music are the inspiration for movement.

Excerpted from Elia 2000, p. 51.

With hopes of becoming a famous ballerina, Simonson moved to New York City at age 18. The rigorous training, rehearsal, and audition schedule caused continuous injuries. A severe injury finally stopped her. While recuperating, she studied anatomy and realized that she had to change how she was working her body. She retrained her muscles and, through her understanding of how the body works, took her first step toward developing her well-known style. Simonson's holistic approach to training involves caring for the body and working within the parameters of the body's possibilities and limitations. Lynn Simonson teaches at Dance Space Center in New York City.

Did You Know? Training and Retraining

Some coaches and teachers specialize in training and retraining dancers in all technical disciplines. Should you need an expert such as this, be sure to contact an organization like Dance/USA, a national service organization for professional dance, for an expert in your area of study. Or consider attending a certification training program or summer intensive program. Check out *Dance Spirit* magazine's Web site for a listing of opportunities.

CHAPTER 12

Review

Name _____ Class _____ Date _____

Matching
Place all the correct corresponding numbers after each prompt.

Practice:

Storage of information:

Self-confidence:

Retraining:

1.   Relates to how we view ourselves
2.   Requires rewiring
3.   Doesn't always happen automatically
4.   Makes you eager to tackle a challenge
5.   Requires an honest evaluation of the problem
6.   Makes perfect
7.   Occurs when emotional and meaningful connections are made
8.   Makes permanent
9.   Will make you a better learner
10. Is about changing muscle memory
11. Sometimes doesn't make you better at a skill

Short Answers
1.   What real-life school is the *Fame* school modeled after?

2.   What is a lecture/demonstration?

3.   What facts support the idea that Donald McKayle values the importance of passing on his knowledge?

4.   What is the concern with presenting world dance forms on a stage?

Essay
Explain how to find proper training.

 From *Experiencing Dance: From Student to Dance Artist* by H. Scheff, M. Sprague, and S. McGreevy-Nichols, 2005, Champaign, IL: Human Kinetics.

Learning From the Works of Others: Expanding Your Horizons

▶▶▶▶▶▶▶▶▶▶▶▶▶▶▶▶▶▶▶▶▶

▶▶▶▶▶▶▶▶▶▶▶▶▶▶▶

▶▶▶▶▶▶▶▶▶▶▶▶▶▶▶

From chapter 13 you will

1. learn how to respond to the works of others;

2. use the responding process to improve your choreography; and

3. use the responding process to improve your performance.

Adapted, by permission, from Steward Photography. © 2003

Famous dancers and choreographers often credit artists who have preceded them. Many young artists not only create their own style but are also influenced by those earlier dancers and choreographers. They observe and learn, and they modify and create a new version of immediate and long-term history.

►LESSON 13.1

Viewing, Analyzing, and Critiquing the Works of Others

5,6,7,8 Move It!

Observe a dance phrase. Write a reflection on the dance phrase and anything else that it made you think about.

Vocabulary

responding • objective • subjective

Curtain Up

"The critic is someone who expresses a reasoned opinion on any matter involving a judgment of value, truth, or righteousness; the opinion may also be an appreciation of the work's beauty, technique, or interpretation" (Schrader 1996, p. 174). The work of a critic responding to a work of art is also useful for dance students. Many standards, high school exit requirements, and national arts assessments expect dance students to create, perform, and respond. Critiquing another person's work can also be used to improve a dancer's performance and a choreographer's dance work.

Responding to dance requires observing, analyzing, and reporting in written or oral mode. Experience and practice are necessary for improving skill in responding to dances. To be a good observer of a dance, one needs to have an open mind and the ability to stifle personal aesthetic preferences and feelings.

A good observer needs to be aware of one's own biases. First, objectively observe what is happening in a dance. How is it put together and what kind of steps and movements do the dancers use? Then reflect and interact with the dance work. It is almost like having a conversation with the dance. Two methods for interact-

▶ You and your peers can help each other.

ing with a dance are to write your reflections in a notebook and to have a conversation with another viewer of the dance. Both objective (factual) and subjective (personal feelings or thoughts) responses are valid here. Use these responses as data to further analyze and design a critique of the dance. A full critique includes the following:

- Description of the dance. What did the dancers do? What did the work look like? How was the dance mechanically put together?
- Interpretation. What was communicated? What does the dance mean?
- Evaluation. Was the dance good, mediocre, or poor? Does it make sense? Is it of value, and is it meaningful? Does it move you? Why? How does it achieve this? Support opinions with reasons and details from the dances.
- Context of the work. How does the dance connect to past dances and history and to current trends of the society and the choreographer's other work?

The same process is useful in critiquing a peer's work. Viewing, analyzing, and critiquing a peer's work are helpful to both of you. The critiquing process is double-edged, and a critique of a performance or piece of choreography can help all involved improve their work.

Take the Stage

Learning to respond to a dance is as important to your development as a dance artist as taking dance classes, performing, and choreographing. Developing your critical and evaluative thinking will improve your abilities in both performing and choreographing. Complete the following activity to gain experience in responding:

1. Observe a dance (preferably a live performance).
2. Write a first draft of a critique by
   - describing the dance,
   - interpreting the meaning of the dance,
   - evaluating the dance, and
   - placing the dance in a context.

Take a Bow

Rewrite the draft as a final copy of the critique.

Spotlight: John Martin and Walter Terry

John Martin (1893-1985) and Walter Terry (1913-1982) were both dance critics for two major newspapers at the same period in history. John Martin worked for the *New York Times,* and Walter Terry worked for the *New York Herald Tribune.* The two men had very different styles of writing and opinions about the same dance works and dancers. Neither was trained in dance, but both were devoted to dance as an art form and to the people who made dance happen. Most of their reviews are preserved in books and library archives. The two men also published books on the subject of dance.

Did You Know? Career As a Dance Critic

Preparing for a career as a dance critic can be daunting. Many dance critics do not earn a living just by reviewing and critiquing dance. Only big-city newspapers can afford to keep one person as a full-time dance critic. Remarkably, a great portion of dance critics are not former dancers, nor do they have a basic dance education. Many are good writers who might have an appreciation of dance and dancers. Many, from smaller towns and cities, have other responsibilities to the newspaper or magazine or they are freelance critics. Large dance institutions have given crash courses and seminars for the edification of working dance critics. These seminars are designed to make the critics aware of techniques for watching, reporting, and reflecting on a dance performance.

Works of Others Influencing Your Choreography

5,6,7,8 **Move It!**

Watch another student's dance study, section of a dance, or completed dance. Analyze the dance to identify the most important qualities. Make a short, solo dance study based on these qualities. You now have added to your choreographic range by learning from the work of another.

Vocabulary

artisan

Curtain Up

Have you ever come out of a dance concert just itching to get into a dance studio? The audience was enthralled and moved. How did the choreographer construct the dance to communicate so well? What was it about the form, structure, composition, and style that made the choreography work?

The ability to observe a dance and use critical skills to analyze it (respond) will help you improve as a choreographer. In medieval times, young apprentices worked and learned from artisans (master craftspeople or artists). Today, in addition to composition teachers, live concerts and videotaped performances can help young choreographers improve their art. Taking a dance apart will help you better understand the choreographic process.

If you're evaluating another's work to relate it to your work or life experiences, "then it is appropriate to respond personally and to consider the ways in which you were affected by the piece, the things you liked or did not like, you would have done differently, you admired, and so on" (Schrader 1996, p.173). Keep the focus of the critique on the work and not on the choreographer, especially if you are critiquing a peer.

Spotlight: Dancing Wheels

Dancing Wheels is a premier modern dance company that employs stand-up and sit-down (wheelchair-bound) dancers in the movement and choreography. The company has toured nationally. They inspire people, with and without disabilities, to integrate people with different abilities into a homogeneous performing group. The company often invites choreographers to work with them. In their repertoire they have short concert pieces as well as full, evening-length works. They have appeared on television and at benefit performances as well as in their own concert tours. To find out more about Dancing Wheels, you can use the search words "Dancing Wheels Company" or read *Dancing Wheels* by Patricia McMahon, published by Houghton Mifflin.

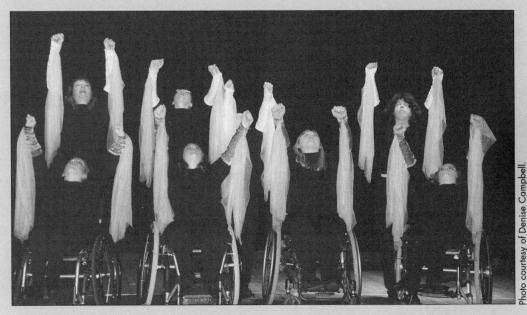

Photo courtesy of Denise Campbell.

▶ Meaningful Movements Dance Company celebrates all abilities!

Take the Stage

As you develop into a dance artist, you will gain wisdom and experience from seeing other choreographers' work. Artwork can inspire other new artwork. This activity will demonstrate this fact.

1. Observe a dance (live or videotaped).

2. Analyze the dance according to choreographic forms, elements, styles, and qualities.

3. Choose one aspect of the analysis.

4. Create a dance study based on this one aspect.

 Take a Bow

Write a reflection on this dance study and what you learned from this lesson. What aspects of this choreographer's work will help you improve your choreography?

 Did You Know? Very Special Arts

Very Special Arts (or VSA) is an international organization that supports and promotes the arts for people with disabilities. They work with children and adults and have representation in most states. Sometimes they are linked with Special Olympics. They organize festivals and award ceremonies. This is not only for dance but for all arts as well. Look in your phone book for the office nearest you. This might be a great place to do an internship.

 ►Lesson 13.3

Improving Your Performance by Watching Others

5,6,7,8 **Move It!**

During a technique class, watch how the best jumpers or turners (or those who excel at any other skill) organize and use their bodies. If there is time, ask them for helpful hints. Try to use the new knowledge to improve your skill.

 Vocabulary

rapport

Curtain Up

All great performers have their reasons for being at the top of their field. A dancer may be in top physical condition or particularly expressive. A dancer may have an awareness, projection, and rapport (connection) with the audience. The dancer may have spent many years studying with a particular teacher or company school and can execute a certain dance form or style perfectly. A dancer may have a specific talent that seems superhuman to the public. (The great Nijinsky was said to have an unbelievable ability to hang in the air during jumps.)

You can analyze all of these performance aspects and even apply some of them to your work as a performer. As with choreography, a master's work, once analyzed, has great value to the younger apprentice. Watch how the experienced dancers use the movement elements and Laban effort actions. You should see clarity of intent and physical function. Neither energy nor movement is wasted. Look at the technique and physical capabilities. For example, how does this dancer use her pliés? Masterful performers are aware of manipulating space. They can get caught up in the relations and narratives inherent in the choreography. There is a melding of the performer's personal voice and that of the choreographer's.

No one lives in a vacuum. We can learn something of value from everyone. Dancers are not exceptions to this principle. We have much to learn from each other, whether we are watching world-famous stars in a full production or our peers in a dance class. Be observant. Describe, interpret, evaluate, and place this performance in the context of your life's situation. A word of caution: Emulation is fine, but cloning is not. Do not undervalue your unique and powerful voice as an artist. Watch. Analyze. Evaluate. Keep what is useful to you, and discard what is not.

Take the Stage

Observing master performers and technicians will inspire you to work toward improving your artistry. This activity demonstrates this fact.

1. Choose one aspect of technique or performance that you would like to improve on. During one of the dances in a concert, focus on the performer who best uses this skill. Analyze how the performer is achieving this aspect.

2. During your own practice session, try to apply what you learned to your technique or performance.

Take a Bow

During a dance class, share what you learned. Take notes on what the other students discovered (your teacher may provide you with a handout). Apply these tips to your work.

Spotlight: Jerome Robbins

Jerome Robbins' (1918-1998) use of different dance forms in each of his works attests to his own versatility and dance education. He was equally comfortable in choreographing for ballet, musical comedy, modern, and ethnic dance forms as well as for stage, film, and television. When he died in 1998, his personal archives were bequeathed to the New York Library for the Performing Arts. He used his dancers in the process of making his dances. He also had his dancers observe what they were to perform. When staging *Fiddler On The Roof* he had the dancers attend Hassidic weddings. When working on a reconstruction of one of his dances from a Broadway show, he had the dancers study the original script of the whole show so that the individual piece would be performed with the integrity of the original.

Did You Know? Broadway Shows Using Different Dance Styles

Broadway is home to many shows that use ethnic, cultural, and world dance as a basis for the choreography. Some that come to mind are *Fiddler on the Roof; Flower Drum Song; The King and I; Candide; West Side Story; Zorba; Aida; The Lion King; Riverdance;* and *Bring in da Noise, Bring in da Funk.* Dancers are asked to observe performances and videos of the selected dance forms before they start learning the choreography.

►Many shows like *The King and I* use dance forms other than Western dance.

CHAPTER 13

Review

Name _____ Class _____ Date _____

Matching

Place the letter of the correct answer in the blank.

1. Focus on the dance ___
2. Objective means ___
3. Subjective means ___
4. Opinions should be supported with ___
5. Interacting with a dance is like a ___

(a) reasons and details

(b) factual information

(c) conversation

(d) personal feelings or thoughts

(e) as a whole

Fill in the Blank

1. In medieval times _____ worked for and learned from master craftspeople.
2. Taking a dance _____ will help you better understand the _____.
3. Keep the _____ of the critique on the _____ and not on the _____.
4. Experienced dancers should have a clarity of intent and _____ _____.
5. You have a unique and powerful _____ as an _____.

Essay

Write about the process of improving your work as a performer and a choreographer by observing and analyzing the dance work of others.

Strutting Your Stuff: Sharing Your Art Form

▶▶▶▶▶▶▶▶▶▶▶▶▶▶▶▶▶▶▶▶▶▶

▶▶▶▶▶▶▶▶▶▶▶▶▶▶▶▶

▶▶▶▶▶▶▶▶▶▶▶▶▶▶▶

From chapter 14 you will

1. learn how to create a public presentation;

2. learn how to research your community for venues for sharing; and

3. learn the importance of sharing your art form through mentoring and community service.

►Overture

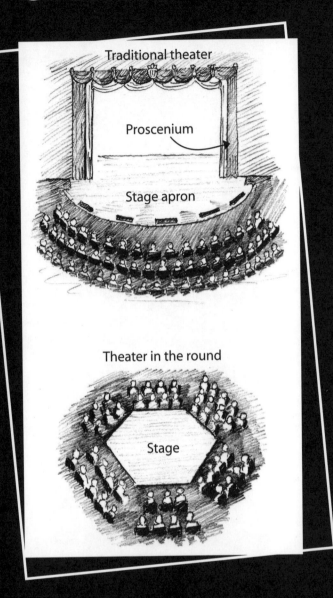

Traditional theater

Proscenium

Stage apron

Theater in the round

Stage

A performance needs an audience. A performer needs to share her art. The performance or exhibition can be formal or informal. It can be in a theater, an auditorium, a grange hall, a school cafeteria, a gymnasium, a field house, or the great outdoors. There are ideal and not-so-ideal performance venues (places where performances take place). Dancers need a venue that has a safe floor. It might not always be a raised stage with a perfect sprung floor or with a marley surface. They can't always be fussy about where that sharing takes place. Dancers, through the years, have learned to acclimate to various venues, sharing and passing on what they know and can do through community outreach and mentoring.

Creating and Planning Presentations for Specific Venues

5,6,7,8 Move It!

Create a dance phrase that would be appropriate for a senior center performance. Create a dance phrase that would be appropriate for a kindergarten class to watch.

Vocabulary

wings • masking

Curtain Up

You have a dance or collection of dances. Now you need to locate a venue, a place and audience, for a performance. Not all dances are appropriate for all audiences. To keep audience interest, you may need to tailor the presentation to the special audience. In a high school exit exhibition or senior concert, you would choose your most accomplished works and a more formal performance space. For a group of kindergartners, a lively, fast-paced, colorful presentation will stand a better chance of keeping the audience's attention.

Some venues will require that you change your costuming, footwear, and possibly some choreography to fit in the space. Some venues present such problems as uneven floors, superheated floors from the sun, lack of changing areas, and small amounts of dance space. It would be wise to get the dimensions of the dance or stage area so that you can rehearse your piece in the available space. Some venues do not include wings. Wings are curtains or flats that provide masking, a cover that hides the performers from the view of the audience. If this masking does not exist for crossovers, your dancers must practice standing quietly at the sides of the dance space and possibly change exits and choreography to accommodate for this lack of masking. Other changes in the choreography may be necessary for the protection of the dancers. For example, knee slides are not recommended for a splintering wood floor or on a hill in a park. Costumes should be appropriate to the venue as well. If no changing areas are provided, a basic underlay costume can be changed in appearance by layering different costume pieces over it.

If the venue has limited or no lighting capabilities (as a cafetorium in an elementary school), then a dance that needs high-tech lighting effects would not be a wise choice for your programming. It would be wise in this case to choose more movement-oriented pieces. Always ask whether the sound system will be provided and what type of technology is being used (CDs or tapes). Even if the sound system is provided, it is always advisable to bring your own backup. If there is no microphone available, and the space is large or in a large outdoor space, avoid pieces that use text and narration. However, if a microphone is available or the space is small enough so that you can be heard without amplification, some inexperienced audiences will find a short explanation before each dance helpful. Finally, when performing at venues or sites other than one you are used to, be flexible and ready for anything.

Photo courtesy of Michael Gendreau.

► Outdoor venues are often challenging.

Take the Stage

Good preparation is essential for taking your show on the road. Follow these suggestions:

1. Either alone or in a group, design dance performance programming that would be appropriate for a particular audience. (Some examples of audiences are young children, peers, senior citizens, general public, and dance-knowledgeable audiences.)

2. Consider all the possible variables in lesson 14.1 Curtain Up as you choose your dances, costumes, footwear, and accompaniment. You should keep these variables in mind when you create your program.

Take a Bow

Create a short narrative that describes and promotes your presentation. Be sure to describe the audiences that would benefit from and enjoy this presentation, and support why this is so. (In preparation for lesson 14.2 Take the Stage, this information can be presented in flyer format.)

Spotlight: Virginia Tanner

Information adapted from www.alumni.utah.edu/continuum/spring97/vdt.html.

Virginia Tanner was affiliated with the University of Utah. She developed and ran a huge children's program, but she also had many students as part of her Creative Dance and Children's Dance Theatre (CDT) that has since become a Utah institution. The fact that this program has grown over its more than 50-year history is a credit to Ms. Tanner's ability to choreograph to her students' abilities and present material that inspired the student audience. CDT performs (under the direction of Mary Ann Lee since 1979) for more than 40,000 Utah residents each year and has made appearances as far away as Washington, D.C. and Malaysia. Not only do they entertain but they also present lecture/demonstrations and teacher and community workshops as educational components of their work.

Did You Know? MTV's Tina Landon

MTV has become a home for many choreographers in several genres. One of the most prolific has been Tina Landon. She really knows her audience. The list of her accomplishments in the choreographing of music videos, commercials, and trade shows is very long. The variety of people with whom she has worked is equally long, including Britney Spears, Jennifer Lopez, and Christina Aguilera. She just knows how to get to and please her audience.

►Lesson 14.2

Finding Places in the Community to Share Your Dance Presentation

5,6,7,8 Move It!

Walk or drive around your community and take note of venues that could host a dance performance. If possible, arrange to visit the inside of these venues to determine the specifics of the venue. (If actual traveling is not possible, then brainstorm on possible venues with your classmates.)

Vocabulary

proscenium • pas de deux • presenters • booked

Curtain Up

When people first think about dance performances, they usually envision a plush auditorium with a proscenium, which is a stage with a formal arch at the front that clearly separates the performers from the audience. For some audiences and dancers, such a large-scale setting is not feasible. It is often advisable for the dancers to go out into the community to look for more unique venues. Often the unusual sites produce the best experiences for both the performers and the audiences. Imagine the thrill of a preschooler who has the experience of seeing a tap dancer performing in the classroom, or the excitement of a senior citizen who has just seen a ballet pas de deux (dance for two) performed in the recreation room. What better way to open an outdoor festival or school field day than to have a company of African drummers and dancers lead an opening procession!

When you talk about matching your site with your work you can find no better example than the opening ceremonies of the 2002 Salt Lake City Winter Olympics, which were a blending of spectacle, pomp, tradition, and dance. The whole event was planned and staged by Kenny Ortega. He was asked to come up with an event that was a mixture of history, tradition, and emotion. For those people in the stadium and for those watching on television, it was just that. To Mr. Ortega's credit, he used many local dance groups, including those from Brigham Young University, in the opening ceremonies, closing ceremonies, and in other ceremonies that the TV audience was not privileged to see. Mr. Ortega won an Emmy for his direction of that event. He also was awarded the Golden Eagle Award for lifetime achievement from Nosotros, an organization founded by Ricardo Montalbán to improve the image of Hispanics in the entertainment industry (www.schwartzmanpr.com/agency/kennyortega.asp).

To locate alternative venues, research not only physical sites but also school, community, and government groups that act as presenters or sponsors of activities, festivals, and holiday ceremonies and celebrations. Partnerships among community, school, and arts organizations will often lead to performance opportunities. Once your group gets booked, or asked to perform, word of mouth will usually bring in more opportunities. Try to accommodate and adapt to the specific needs and limitations of each site, but realize that not all opportunities may be feasible.

Take the Stage

Being organized and prepared will help you present your work at different venues.

1. Using the flyer or promotional document that you created in lesson 14.1 Take a Bow, call, visit, or mail your information to appropriate venues.

2. Once you have agreed on the booking, use the Booking Checklist on page 191 to make sure that you have dealt with all the necessary details and preparations. Make sure that you have completed a signed contract with the presenter or venue manager.

Take a Bow

Perform. Evaluate and write about the success of your performance experience. Include all parts of the process such as booking, contact and communication, venue description and necessary adaptations, description of the performing experience, and audience reactions.

Spotlight: Liz Lerman

Reprinted by permission of the Dance Exchange.

From classes at the age of five through a masters degree in dance from George Washington University, Liz Lerman received a thorough grounding in classical ballet and modern technique from such leaders in the field of dance as Ethel Butler, Viola Farber, Peter Saul, Jan Van Dyke, Maida Withers, and Twyla Tharp. Wanting to expand her expressive range and social applications of her work, she embarked on an exploration of a variety of additional aesthetic and theatrical traditions. After a period in New York, Liz moved to Washington where she founded the Liz Lerman Dance Exchange in 1976. Her credentials include an American Choreographer Award and numerous Choreography Fellowships from the National Endowment for the Arts. Liz's work has been commissioned by Lincoln Center, American Dance Festival, Dancing in the Streets, BalletMet, and the Kennedy Center. She has received an American Choreographer Award, the American Jewish Congress Golda Award, the first annual Pola Nirenska Award, the Mayor's Art Award, and *Washingtonian Magazine's* Washingtonian of the Year Award.

Combining dance with realistic imagery, her works are defined by the spoken word, drawing from literature, personal experience, philosophy, and political and social commentary. Ms. Lerman is a frequent keynote speaker and panelist for arts and community organizations both nationally and internationally. She is an active participant in Harvard University's Saguarro Seminar. Her book, *Teaching Dance to Senior Adults*, was published in 1983.

Take the Stage: Booking Checklist

Name _____ Class _____ Date _____

Name of venue:

Date and time of performance:

Contact person:

Address (directions):

Telephone:

Fax:

E-mail:

Description of performing space (proscenium, open space, outdoors, raised stage, wings, crossover, dimensions [length and width], lights, sound equipment):

Rest rooms, dressing rooms:

Description of audience and type of presentation or activity:

Contract or letter of agreement needed:

Take the Stage: Agreement or Contract for Booking

Fill in the following information from your interview or meeting with the site manager. Keep for your records.

Name _____ Class _____ Date _____

Name of venue:

Contact information:

Date of performance:

Hours:

Permitted rehearsal hours:

Fees or rentals:

Extra lighting equipment required:

Extra sound equipment required:

Floor composition and care:

Who is responsible for running and upkeep of the following elements:

    Sound:

    Lights:

    Curtain:

    Scene and property shifts:

    Stage management:

    Cleanup:

    Front of house:

    Ticket selling and taking:

    Printing of programs:

Storage capabilities (between rehearsal and performance):

Custodian on duty:

Insurance:

Police or fire deputy requirement (any fee involved and who pays):

Signature of venue manager:_____ Date:_____

Signature of performing organization manager: _____ Date:_____

Did You Know? Dance Teams and Drill Teams

Many high schools across the United States do not have dance programs, but they do have dance teams and drill teams. Some of these teams rehearse during school as part of physical education classes. Some rehearse before or after school. They often support the athletic teams at competitions. They march in parades. They attend competitions designed especially for them. Their costumes vary from the most modest in cost to sequined creations that catch the light and the eyes of the judges. Most teams require an audition (tryout) to become a member. Because of this fact, there are many preteams where potential members can get the practice and learn the traditional moves. Dancers are now asked if they have any training in jazz, ballet, and tap. They have to be flexible and strong and have sparkling personalities. For more information on drill and dance teams, check the Internet.

► Dance teams perform at many community events.

Mentoring and Community Service Through Dance

5,6,7,8 **Move It!**

Find a class of young children. Develop and then teach them a short combination or a warm-up.

Vocabulary

school to work

Curtain Up

In many school districts, community-service and school-to-work programs (internships) are requirements for high school graduation. There is great value in real-world experiences such as internships and volunteer work. For a dance student, this is also true. A dancer has unique talents and skills to offer the community.

As a student, you could do an internship with another public or private school dance program, a professional or regional dance company, or even a private-sector dance school. In addition to learning how all or part of the organization functions, you are furthering your knowledge of the dance field. Make sure that you and your adviser delineate all your roles and responsibilities before the start of your internship.

As an older dance student, you could be an excellent candidate to mentor a younger student. Role models can play an important part in a younger person's life. Think back to a person who took an interest in you when you were younger. Having a mentor to help with school or dance training could be helpful to an elementary school student or even a younger classmate.

Even if your school district does not have community-service or school-to-work opportunities, you can still give back to the community through volunteering. Community clubs and recreation and youth programs (such as Girl Scouts or YMCA programs) are always in need of activities and volunteers. Dancers bring an extra dimension of possibilities to volunteer work in the form of teaching dance classes, choreographing, and lending expertise to small shows.

Take the Stage

The more experience you get as a student, the more prepared you are to gain employment or take advantage of opportunities to further your education.

1. With your teacher, adviser, or guidance counselor, research possible internships, mentoring, or volunteer opportunities.

2. During a preliminary meeting with the site personnel, create a document listing the time frame of tasks and roles and responsibilities of all involved.

Take a Bow

Carry out the internship, mentoring, or volunteer opportunity and keep a daily journal that logs all activities, experiences, and learning. While the day's work is still fresh in your mind, make sure that you write in your journal before you leave your internship site. For the last entry in the log, create a narrative procedure that will be helpful to another student who wishes to participate in a similar project.

Spotlight: Debbie Allen

Debbie Allen (1950-) is a dancer, actor, singer, choreographer, director, and producer. (She is considered a "triple threat" because she dances, sings, and acts.) She has appeared on concert stage, Broadway, television, and movies. But just as important, she sees her role as a mentor and teacher. During the 2003 TV show about young people auditioning for a spot on *Fame*, the audience could see the caring way she handled all the would-be stars, encouraging the ones who needed more time to mature as performers as well as applauding those who were moving on to the top. Debbie Allen also wrote a book that was made into a musical for young audiences. It was commissioned by the Kennedy Center and is titled *Brothers of the Night.*

Did You Know? Internships

Internships can be a helpful and interesting part of your dance education. Most internships do not pay stipends, but sometimes you can get paid for your work. Dance companies of all sizes are looking for help. The dance school where you study may need a student teacher or office staff person. Recreation programs like to have dance people involved, and they might offer internships. Do a Web search using the words "dance internships" or "education internships."

CHAPTER 14

Review

Name _____ Class _____ Date _____

True/False

1. All dances are appropriate for all audiences. _____

2. Changes in the choreography are necessary for the safety of the choreographer. _____

3. You may need to change your dance's costumes for some venues. _____

4. Liz Lerman wrote a book titled *Teaching Dance to Senior Adults*. _____

5. Working for and learning about an organization, such as a dance company, is called a residency. _____

Short Answers

1. Describe how mentoring, volunteering, and internships can be as helpful to the community as they are for the person doing these activities.

2. Describe possible changes in choreography that may be necessary at certain performance venues.

3. Design a program appropriate for a performance for a retirement center's carpeted recreation hall. Describe the costumes, types of dances, and any other aspects necessary for making this presentation successful.

4. Explain how the advice "be flexible and ready for anything" could apply to all the topics in this chapter.

15

Developing Your Portfolio As a Marketing Tool: Next Steps

▶▶▶▶▶▶▶▶▶▶▶▶▶▶▶▶▶▶▶▶▶

▶▶▶▶▶▶▶▶▶▶▶▶▶▶▶▶

Lesson 15.1 Portfolio: A Collection of Your Work

Lesson 15.2 Marketing: Résumé

Lesson 15.3 Auditions

▶▶▶▶▶▶▶▶▶▶▶▶▶▶▶▶

From chapter 15 you will

1. learn how and what to collect for your own portfolio;

2. learn how to market yourself by creating a résumé; and

3. acquire knowledge about what is important at and for an audition.

►Overture

Adapted, by permission, from Steward Photography. © 2003

Once upon a time there was a call in *Variety,* the show-business newspaper, for dancers to come to an audition. The ad did not describe what the show was, just that it was a project. The dancers arrived ready to dance, but dance they did not. They all sat around and discussed their lives as they pertained to dance and what dance meant to them. The dancers agreed to be taperecorded. Then they all left being told that there would be a callback. Those that made the callback arrived ready to dance, but again they sat and talked. On the third callback, they finally danced. Some were chosen and some were not, and that is how *A Chorus Line* was born—a hit Broadway show that told the true stories of the dancers who spoke before they danced. (See lesson 10.3 Spotlight and lesson 15.3 Spotlight for more on this subject.)

Portfolio: A Collection of Your Work

5,6,7,8 Move It!

Create a combination that highlights what you consider your technical strengths. Pair-share (turn to another student and talk about the topic) and give feedback to each other.

Vocabulary

portfolio • body of work • pair share

Curtain Up

When visual artists go for a job interview or to a gallery, they carry with them a portfolio. In this portfolio is a collection of their work. This work is evidence of their capabilities. Dancers, too, can compile evidence of their abilities in portfolio form. Whether you are applying for a job as a dancer or choreographer, seeking admittance into a dance company or college or university dance program, or need to submit evidence of work for a senior project or exit exam, a portfolio can be an important tool that documents and showcases your body of work. Your body of work is your major accomplishments in performance and choreography. When compiling evidence of this work, consider the following categories:

- Accomplishments in dance
  - What do you consider as your major accomplishments during the previous four years?
  - Show that you have been progressing toward your goals in the field.
- Technique training
  - What dance form and style do you consider your best?
  - How much diversity do you possess in various dance forms and styles?

- With whom have you studied?
- What master classes and workshops have you taken?

• Performance
- What kinds of performances have you done?
- Whose choreography have you performed?

• Choreography
- What pieces of choreography have you created?
- Where and by whom has it been performed?
- Have critiques or reviews been written about your work?

• Responding
- Have you written any reviews or critiques, essays, or papers that reveal your knowledge about dance?
- You will need to show evidence of critical-thinking skills and critiquing experience in high school exit requirements or college applications.

• Community service
- Have you ever done any volunteer work that relates to the field of dance?

• Teaching
- Have you taught any classes or workshops?

• References
- Collect evaluations of your work.
- Make a list of people who know your work and might serve as good references.
- Ask them if they would write letters of recommendation.

It is now time to compile documentation that will help support your body of work. Documentation can be in the form of

• recordings (video and audio);
• newspaper clippings;
• photos;
• programs; and
• written documents such as essays, critiques, reflections, and choreographic notes.

Once you have compiled all this material, arrange it in a suitable container. If possible, your portfolio should also be available electronically (on CD-ROM or floppy disk).

Spotlight: Custodians of Dance Legacies

George Balanchine (1904-1983) is regarded as the one of the greatest choreographers in contemporary ballet. His many works are performed by ballet companies all over the world. "Clement Crisp, one of the many writers who eulogized Balanchine, summed up his contribution to the world of ballet: 'It is hard to think of the ballet world without the colossal presence of George Balanchine. . . . But we have not lost Balanchine, not the essential Balanchine, who lives in the great catalogue of masterpieces. . . " (www.nycballet.com/about/nycbgbbio.html). Balanchine's body of work is being preserved under the direction of ballet master-in-chief Peter Martins of the New York City Ballet and the School of American Ballet, which has been designated as the keeper of the Balanchine legacy and ideals. You can learn much more about George Balanchine and the New York City Ballet by using those words in a Web search or by looking up books on the subjects.

Take the Stage

Compile a portfolio that showcases your ability to create, perform, and respond to dance.

 Take a Bow

Share your portfolio with at least three other people. Ask them to evaluate areas in which your portfolio could be improved. Consider your peers' input, and make revisions and additions to your portfolio.

 Did You Know? The Jerome Robbins Dance Division of the New York Public Library for the Performing Arts

From New York Public Library. www.nypl.org/research/lpa/dan/dan.html. Reprinted by permission of the New York Public Library.

The Jerome Robbins Dance Division of the New York Public Library is the largest and most comprehensive archive in the world devoted to the documentation of dance. Chronicling the art of dance in all its manifestations—ballet, ethnic, modern, social, and folk—the division is much more than a library in the usual sense of the word. It is part museum, part film production center, and part consulting service to the professional dance community.

The Jerome Robbins Dance Division keeps the history of dance alive through its collection of films and videotapes, audiotapes, clipping and program files, iconography, and manuscripts and memorabilia.

 **Lesson 15.2**

Marketing: Résumé

5,6,7,8 **Move It!**

With a partner, practice auditioning for each other. Teach each other combinations.

Practice strategies for picking up movements quickly.

 Vocabulary

résumé • head shot

Curtain Up

Now that you have compiled your portfolio, it will be easier for you to develop a résumé. A résumé is a document that tells the person who reads it who you are, what you have accomplished, and what your qualifications are for a certain job or place in a school. The person doing the recruiting sometimes asks for a short biography. You may want to develop more than one document. In one document, you may want to highlight your dance credentials when applying for a position that requires you to dance. In another document, you may want to highlight your administrative experiences when applying for a position in the management end of the field. Just as in your portfolio, the information in a résumé is arranged in categories. See page 202 for a sample format and brief explanation of each of these categories.

Your résumé should be one page long and designed to show off your strengths. The back of the résumé should have your head shot, which is a close-up photograph of your shoulders and head. You should have a professional photographer take your head shot. This can be an expensive process, so be sure to shop around for the best price and quality. You will also need a full-body photo that shows you demonstrating some dance pose. The purpose of this photo is to show body alignment and conditioning, so you should wear proper practice clothing for this photo session. Have this photo ready in case the prospective employer wants to see it. You can also include it in your portfolio.

Take the Stage

Discuss different types of dance jobs, and design your résumé specific to these jobs. Draft a sample résumé and share it with a classmate.

You can use the format in this lesson's Curtain Up as a guide.

Take a Bow

Show your résumé to a dance professional or your guidance counselor. Ask this person to evaluate how well the content and design of the résumé will market your abilities.

Spotlight: James Penrod and Janice Gudde Plastino

In 1970 James Penrod (1934-) and Janice Gudde Plastino published *The Dancer Prepares: Modern Dance for Beginners.* Now in its fifth edition, this book has long served as a primer for students of modern dance. The text begins with a discussion of the nature of modern dance, then it moves on to a consideration of the requirements of a modern dance student in class. Techniques of the genre are detailed in text and diagrams, and information is presented about a dancer's physical health. In addition, a minimal history of modern dance, approaches to choreography, and the process of evaluation are covered. This book is available through major online bookstores.

Curtain Up: Sample Résumé Format

Name:

Contact information:

Address (include city and state):

Phone, e-mail, and fax numbers:

Personal information:

Height: _____ Weight: _____ Hair color: _____ Eye color: _____

Education:

Qualifications (this is a brief summary of why you are qualified for the specific job for which you are applying):

Performing experience (performances, competitions, showcases, productions; list the most recent dates first):

Choreography (your creations should be listed in the following order: the name of the piece and the date [or vice versa], the name of the group that commissioned and performed the piece):

Teaching (teaching credits should be referenced by the sponsoring institution):

Awards (list of any special recognitions that you have received):

Training (list of relevant training, names of teachers, and school or dance forms):

Other experience (any other information that you think will help you give a complete picture of you and your accomplishments):

From *Experiencing Dance: From Student to Dance Artist* by H. Scheff, M. Sprague, and S. McGreevy-Nichols, 2005, Champaign, IL: Human Kinetics.

Did You Know? Professional Résumé Writers

Professional résumé writers will, for a fee, create a résumé for you. They are trained to help you put your best foot forward. These writers can look at your experience and marketable traits and organize the information into a résumé format. If you can't afford this service, many resources (books, software, and Internet sites) are available online. Do an Internet search using the key words "professional résumé writers."

►Lesson 15.3

Auditions

_{5,6,7,}**8 Move It!**

Create a short solo that you could use as an audition piece.

Vocabulary

audition • open audition • callback • charisma •   adjudicator • cattle call • gypsy

Curtain Up

Auditions are a fact of life for a dancer. An audition is the process of competing against others for a job being offered, which can be very rewarding and very stressful. It is best to be as prepared as possible and have a good outlook about the whole process. First do some research about the production, school, program, company, or choreographer that you are auditioning for. Find out what is required so that you go into the audition fully prepared. Show up for the audition well in advance and warm up independently to make sure your specific physical needs are met. Watch and listen. Come to the audition prepared with your résumé and photo. Wear appropriate, conservative dancewear (no thongs or low necklines). Wear tights that have a split foot in case you need to use shoes and go barefoot. Have assorted dance shoes, such as jazz, character, tap, and ballet shoes, in your dance bag. Although you are bound to be nervous, try to stay calm. This is a good time to practice calming breathing techniques.

The purpose of a dance audition is to identify the mental and physical capabilities of the dancers. "Each candidate should be evaluated according to the following criteria: basic comprehension; technical ability (any previous dance training); technical potential; speed of learning; grasp of dynamics (a feel for how the step should look); ability to understand and apply correction and direction; and attitude toward the work and toward others" (Berkson 1990, p. 125). Many times the first audition will be an open audition, in which anyone is welcome to come and try out for a role. Many people usually attend this initial audition (fondly known as a cattle call), which is used to weed out those who do not fit for whatever reason. Those who are invited to a callback are scrutinized more closely. A final callback is when you are asked back so that the adjudicators (auditioners) have an opportunity to look at the remaining group as a whole and make the final selections. Selection at this

► Dancers can participate in many auditions to get a part.

time may depend on dancers' appearance and charisma (personality that is projected while performing) as well as ability. In any audition situation there is a limit to the number of people selected, so don't obsess if you are not chosen.

It is not necessarily because you are not good enough. There are many reasons certain people or combinations of people are chosen. "If at first you don't succeed . . ."

 ## Take the Stage

It is easier to have a new experience when you are among people you know and trust. This is why you should plan a mock audition.

1. Participate in a practice audition. (Obtain help from your teacher or other dance pro-

fessional. They will need to design and run the practice audition.)

2. Break up into small groups and discuss individual experiences. Provide helpful comments to each other on audition behaviors and strategies.

 ## Take a Bow

Reflect on how to improve your audition skills. Determine whether you need additional support or training to improve your chances for a successful audition.

Spotlight: Michael Bennett

Michael Bennett (1943-1987) had a vision. He wanted to tell the story of gypsies (the nickname for Broadway dancers) through song and dance. He went to producer Joseph Papp with his vision. Mr. Papp agreed that it would be a good idea. Presenting it so that it was realistic was the next step in the process of creating a show. When Mr. Bennett got the dancers to the audition, he had them answer questions about their introductions to dance, what brought them to *want* to dance. All these conversations were recorded and used as the basis for the script. Marvin Hamlisch collaborated and created the score for the show, again using the dancers' stories as inspiration. "The Music and the Mirror" is the song of one gypsy alone with her thoughts and passion, the chance to dance. The result was a musical called *A Chorus Line*.

Did You Know? Trade Newspapers

Want to know about job listings and auditions in the entertainment field? Trade newspapers like *The Hollywood Reporter* and *Daily Variety* can keep you informed about auditions and current projects in the field. You might also consider working with an agency. Do a Web search by putting in key words such as "dance newspapers," "theatrical newspapers," or "trade newspapers/dance."

Review

Name _____ Class _____ Date _____

Write a short definition of and give examples for the following words:

1. portfolio—

2. documentation—

3. legacy—

4. audition—

5. résumé—

6. head shot—

7. callback—

Essay

Using these terms, write a procedural narrative that tells a story about a dance student's first audition experience. Be sure to include the information from chapter 15.

▶▶▶ GLOSSARY

AB—A dance phrase (A) followed by a new dance phrase (B).

ABA—A dance phrase (A) followed by a new dance phrase (B) and a return to the first dance phrase (A).

abstract movement—Movement that differs from but is still loosely based on the literal movement.

accented beat—The beat that gets the emphasis.

accented beats—Changing the emphasis on which beat gets the accent.

accumulation—A choreographic form in which there is a distinct movement or dance phrase, then different movement or dance phrases are added to the original phrase and subsequent phrases.

adjudicator—An auditioner.

aesthetic—Pertaining to a sense of the beautiful and a philosophical theory or idea of what is artistically valid at a given time.

affect—The conscious, subjective aspect of an emotion.

air patterns—Dancers' pathways in the air as they move through space.

alignment—Proper, functional posture.

allegro—Fast, quick-footed movement.

antagonist—A muscle that counteracts or slows down a motion.

anterior iliac superior—The anterior extremity of the iliac crest, which provides attachment for the inguinal ligament and the sartorius muscle.

apprentice—A person who works alongside a mentor and learns directly from the mentor. The apprentice then goes out on one's own to work in dance performance, education, or other dance-related fields.

artisans—Master artists or craftspeople.

assemblé—An elevated move, leaving the floor from one foot and landing on two feet.

asymmetrical—Different shapes on both sides of the body or on both sides of a formation.

audition—A process in which dancers compete against each other for the available positions.

ballon—Elevation.

Bartenieff Fundamentals—A series of exercises built on the work of Rudolf Laban.

battement—A simple kick.

battens —Poles above the stage from which lights, scenery, and drapes can be hung.

beginning, middle, and end—A basic choreographic form; a dance should have a beginning shape or pose or entrance, a middle consisting of development or exploration of the main idea, and a clear ending consisting of a shape, pose, or exit.

Bloom's taxonomy—A hierarchy of six levels of the complexity of human thinking.

Bob Fosse—Broadway and Hollywood choreographer known for his own technique and style of jazz dance.

body language—The whole body tells its own story in movement while standing, sitting, walking, being awake, or sleeping.

body of work—A dancer's major accomplishments in performance and choreography.

booked—Asked to perform.

Bournonville—A codified ballet technique begun in Denmark.

Broadway ballet—A dance section that promotes the flavor of the production but doesn't necessarily have anything to do with the show.

Butoh—A postmodern movement in Japan.

call and response—One person moves, and the other person's movement responds (answers) the movement of the initial mover.

callback—When a dancer is asked to return for another audition.

canon—A musical or dance structure in two or more parts. The main phrase is imitated by the successive dancers at successive intervals. Also known as round.

cattle call—An affectionate name for open audition.

chance dance—A choreographic form that can be described as a series of dance phrases that are performed in a random order. Each time the dance is done, it is in a different order and has a different appearance.

charisma—Personality.

Charles Weidman—Modern dancer and teacher who, along with Doris Humphrey, developed the Humphrey-Weidman technique.

choreographic processes—Methods used to enhance and carry the dance forward.

collage—Choreographic form that consists of a series of movement phrases that are often unrelated but have been brought together to create a single dance with a beginning, a middle, and an end.

complementary—Different but related shapes, movement, or dance phrases. An example is making a different shape out of curves to complement an original curved shape.

concentric contraction—Shortening of a muscle in a movement.

concert dance—Dance company performance.

connectivity, body–half—Connection between the whole right side and whole left side of the body.

connectivity, core–distal—Connection between the center of the body and the ends of the limbs.

connectivity, cross–lateral—Connection between the right side which crosses oppositionally to the left side, or contralateral relationships.

connectivity, head–tail—Connection between the head and tailbone.

connectivity, upper–lower—Connection between the upper body and lower body.

contrast—Opposite movement.

copy—Repeat movement.

critique—Corrections and comments.

cue to cue—Rehearsals in which the music, sound, curtain, and light cues are run from the beginning of the show through the final curtain without the dancers.

dance class etiquette—Limited conversation, focus on the teacher and corrections, and proper use of personal space.

dance coach—A person who helps a performer perfect the details of a role.

dance company school—Usually affiliated with a professional dance company.

dance study—Exploration of an idea through the creation of a short dance.

dance triplet—Basic waltz step in which the dancer steps forward on the right foot while bending the knee, moves the left foot forward on the ball of the foot, then steps forward on the ball of the right foot. The rhythm is down, up, up.

demi-plié—A knee bend in which the dancer keeps the knees over the toes.

Doris Humphrey—Modern dancer and teacher who, along with Charles Weidman, developed the Humphrey-Weidman technique.

downtime—The time it takes to set the new learning by organizing and coordinating the movements and the timing within the brain.

eccentric contraction—Lengthening of a muscle.

elevation—Height of an airborne move.

endorphins—Mood-elevating hormones.

Enrico Cecchetti—Developer of a codified ballet technique begun in Europe and used worldwide today.

exhibition—Any performance, anytime you appear before an audience of any size.

extension—Straightening or increasing the angle between two bones.

facings—The stage directions to which the dancers perform their movements.

fall—Movement ending on the ground.

five Ws—The where, when, what, why, and who of a performance (for press releases).

fixator—Muscle that holds a body part in a particular position to support the movement of another body part.

flat—A sheet of plywood or a wooden frame covered with canvas that can be painted.

flexion—Bending or decreasing the angle between two bones.

floor pattern—Dancers' pathways on the floor as they move through space.

focal point—Where the audience looks.

footsteps—Arthur Murray designed instruction books using little outlined feet that he called footsteps.

formation—Where dancers stand in relation to other dancers.

gel—The cellophane-like material that goes in front of the lighting instrument to produce colored light.

George Balanchine—Developer of a codified ballet technique begun in Russia and based on Vaganova but defined even more when he came to the United States and then developed New York City Ballet and its repertoire.

ground bass—A group of dancers repeats a series of simple movements while, in front, a smaller number of dancers (or soloist) performs a contrasting, often more complex dance phrase.

gypsy—A nickname for a Broadway dancer.

habits of mind—Thinking skills or behaviors that help us function in all types of learning situations.

head shot—A photograph of the head and shoulders.

hoofer—Tap dancer, vaudevillian dancer.

hyperextended knee—When the knee pushes back beyond proper alignment of the bones of the upper and lower leg.

hyperextension—Going beyond straightening.

imagery—Taking oneself through mental practice.

improvise—Move without preplanning.

Isadora Duncan—Sometimes termed "the mother of modern dance."

isolation—Moving one body part without moving any other part.

kinesiologist—One who studies the principles of mechanics and anatomy in relation to human movement.

kinesphere—Making one's own space.

kinesthetic—Movement skill.

kyphosis-lordosis—A condition in which the spine has an exaggerated S shape when viewed from the side.

Laban effort actions—Combinations of three of the effort elements:

dab—Uses light weight, sudden time, and direct space.

flick—Uses light weight, sudden time, and indirect space.

float—Uses light weight, sustained time, and indirect space.

glide—Uses light weight, sustained time, and direct space.

press—Uses strong weight, sustained time, and direct space.

punch—Uses strong weight, sudden time, and direct space.

slash—Uses strong weight, sudden time, and indirect space.

wring—Uses strong weight, sustained time, and indirect space.

Laban efforts—The attitudes toward the energy that is exerted when doing a movement:

flow—Attitude toward flow is bound (controlled) or free (uncontrolled).

space—Attitude toward space is direct (the movement has a single focus) or indirect (the movement has many foci).

time—Attitude toward time is sudden (showing urgency or anxiety) or sustained (showing a relaxed, easygoing feeling).

weight—Attitude toward weight is strong (expending much energy) or light (using a fine or delicate touch).

Labanalysis—One way of observing and describing movement (a system created by Rudolph Laban and his followers).

learn to learn—Learning to adapt one's own learning style to any subject.

lecture/demonstration—A presentation that combines a lecture on a specific topic with a demonstration that highlights the main points of the information.

Lester Horton—Dancer, choreographer, and developer of his own technique for modern dance.

levels—High, middle, and low.

ligament—Tissue that connects bones to bones.

Lindy hop—Dance first popular in the 1920s; also known as the jitterbug.

literal movement—Exact, real-life movement.

locomotor movement—Traveling movement.

lordosis—Abnormal curvature of the spine forward; swayback posture.

Luigi—Innovative creator of his own technique and style of jazz dance.

madrigal dance—Dances fashionable during the 16th century and later, done in Italy, France, and England.

mark—Move through steps without using the full space or energy.

Martha Graham—Modern dancer and choreographer whose company still exists to perpetuate her work.

masking—Cover for performers to get from one place to another behind the scenes.

master class—Taught by teachers who are ranked at the top of their field, hence the title of master.

Matt Mattox—Innovative creator of his own technique and style of jazz dance.

metacognition—Thinking about thinking.

motif and development—A choreographic form described as a brief movement phrase that is stated or danced and then developed into a full-blown dance or section of a dance.

mounting a production—Putting together all the pieces that go into a show and getting it up on the stage.

movement patterns—Habitual ways of moving.

Muganda dance—A dance from Zambia that is an example of dance as a means of social commentary.

multiple intelligences—Dr. Howard Gardner's theory that people think and are intelligent in different ways. No one uses only one kind of intelligence, but rather, people usually use a combination of these ways of thinking.

muscle memory—The nervous and muscular systems will develop a type of recall after repeating a movement many times.

muse—A mythical goddess.

narrative—A story line.

nature versus nurture—Refers to traits that are inherited and traits that are learned.

neuron—A nerve cell in the brain.

nonfiction—Themes taken from history, current events, or social issues.

nonlocomotor movement—Movement that stays in place. Also called axial movement.

objective—Factual.

on the bias—Fabric that is cut on a diagonal instead of straight up and down.

open auditions—Everyone is welcome to try out.

overmuscling—Straining a movement, which could be damaging.

overtraining—Not allowing muscles to recuperate adequately. With overtraining, a dancer can actually break down muscle tissue rather than develop it.

pair-share—Turn to a partner and talk about a topic.

pas de bourrée—A three-step movement: Step behind the left foot with the right foot, step to open with left, step in front with right.

pas de deux—A dance for two.

passive stretching—A partner takes the muscle through the stretched range of motion while the person being stretched remains passive. This should be done carefully because the person stretching the muscle can't feel when the muscle reaches the overstretched point.

petit allegro—Rapid footwork as part of the requirement for a Balanchine dancer.

plastic—Able to change.

poignant—A moving and touching emotional feeling.

port de corps—A high release or back bend.

port de bras—Carriage of the arms.

portfolio—A collection of work.

potpourri—None of the pieces in a dance performance relates to another in theme or style.

practice—Learners repeating a skill over time.

presenters—Sponsors.

prime mover—A muscle that is mainly responsible for a motion.

proscenium—A formal arch at the front of the stage that clearly separates the performers from the audience.

range of motion—Amount of mobility and ease of movement.

rapport—Connection with the audience.

rehearsal—What performing artists call practice.

resistance—A type of exercise in which one person does a movement while another person presses or pulls the body part in the opposite direction.

responding—Observing, analyzing, and reporting in written or oral mode.

résumé—A document that contains all the information that a performer wants people to know about her.

RICE—Acronym meaning rest, ice, compression, and elevation; a way to allow healing to occur.

rondo—A choreographic pattern in which A is the primary movement phrase and is constantly being repeated and interspersed between others. B, C, and D should be different from each other and from A.

Royal Academy of Dance (RAD)—A codified ballet technique based in Great Britain with a syllabus and set of exams.

rubric—A listing of requirements that should be included in a work; the rubric also assigns a score.

Ruth St. Denis—One of the pioneers of modern dance.

school to work—Internship.

self-concept—The way a person views oneself.

shape—Position.

sissonne—A jump from two feet and landing on one foot.

static stretching—The muscle to be stretched is lengthened slowly by staying in a fairly comfortable position for 15 to 30 seconds. When the feeling of stretching subsides, the person stretching can move into a deeper stretch position.

strike—Take the show apart.

strip lights—Light bulbs (called lamps) mounted in a long, metal box with dividers for each one.

subjective—Personal feelings or thoughts.

sweat equity—Hard work.

symmetrical—The same on both sides.

synergist—A muscle that often helps a prime mover.

synovial joint—Includes cartilage (a form of connective tissue that is smooth and elastic), covered bone endings, and a capsule (also made up of connective tissue) that protect and strengthen the joints; synovial fluid lubricates the joint (like oil in an engine).

tapestry—A woven wall hanging that depicts a scene.

tempo—The speed of music or dance.

tendon—Connects a muscle to a bone.

Terpsichore—The muse of dance.

theatrical dance—A dance created with the audience in mind.

theme and variation—A dance phrase or section of a dance with subsequent dance phrases or sections that are variations of the original.

theme-based—All the dances are about one subject.

tour en l'air—A 360-degree turn in the air.

trade show—A minishow that advertises products.

transfer—Taking new learning from one situation and applying it to another situation.

transition—Movement that links one element to another.

triple threat—Proficiency in dancing, singing, and acting.

tutu—Skirt of a ballet dancer.

types of joints:

ball and socket—Hip and shoulder joint.

ellipsoid—Wrist and ankle.

gliding—Wrist and ankle.

hinge—Knee, elbow, fingers, and toes.

pivot—Top of the neck.

saddle—Thumb.

types of movements:

abduction—Moving away from the midline of the body.

adduction—Moving toward the midline of the body.

circumduction—Combination of flexion, extension, adduction, and abduction; this seems like a full circling.

depression—Pressing downward.

elevation—Lifting.

eversion—Sideways movement sliding outward.

extension—Straightening or increasing the angle between two bones.

flexion—Bending or decreasing the angle between two bones.

hyperextension—Going beyond straightening.

inversion—Sideways movement sliding inward.

inward rotation—Turning in.

outward rotation—Turning out.

unison—All moving at the same time and doing the same movement in the same way.

up full—Lights up to maximum capacity.

Vaganova—A codified ballet technique that originated in Russia; other techniques are based on this technique.

venue—A place for a performance.

vernacular—Popular style.

weight sharing—Guiding, giving, and taking weight from another dancer.

wings—Curtains or flats that provide masking.

world dance—Dances that stem from within an ethnic culture and express the movement aesthetic of that culture.

►►► REFERENCES, BIBLIOGRAPHY, AND SUGGESTED READINGS

Allen, Debbie. 1999. *Brothers of the night*. New York: Penguin Putnam.

American Ballet Theatre. Bio of Jennifer Tipton. www.abt.org/education/archive/designers/tipton_j.html (accessed January 2004).

American Dance Festival. Erick Hawkins. www.americandancefestival.org/Archives/scripps/hawkins.html (accessed January 2004).

Art and Culture Network. Lar Lubovitch. www.artandculture.com/arts/artist?artistId=701 (accessed January 2004).

Arts Education Partnership. Champions of change: The impact of arts on learning. http://aep-arts.org/Champions.html (accessed January 2004).

Arts Education Partnership. Critical links: Learning in the arts and students' academic and social development. http://aep-arts.org/CLTemphome.html (accessed January 2004).

Bader, Victoria (producer). Flight: Caught. Interview with David Parsons for PBS series EGG: The Arts Show. www.pbs.org/wnet/egg/203/caught/index.html (accessed January 2004).

Balanchine, George. June 1954. Ballet for your children. *Dance Magazine*.

Banes, Sally. 1994. *Writing dancing in the age of postmodernism*. Hanover, NH: University Press of New England.

Bartenieff, Irmgard, with Lewis, Dori. 1980. *Body movement: Coping with the environment*. New York: Gordon and Breach Science.

Bentley, Toni. *Costumes by Karinska*. www.tonibentley.com/pages/karinska_pages/karinska_excerpt3.html (accessed January 2004).

Berson, Robert. 1990. *Musical theatre choreography: A practical method for preparing and staging dance in a musical show (stage and costume)*. New York: Backstage Books.

Billman, Larry. 1997. *Fred Astaire: A bio-biography*. Westport, CT: Greenwood Press.

Bloom, B.S. 1956. *Taxonomy of educational objectives, handbook 1: Cognitive domain*. New York: McGraw-Hill.

Bremser, Martha, ed. 1999. *Fifty contemporary choreographers*. New York: Routledge.

Brown, Jean Morrison, ed. 1979. *The vision of modern dance*. Princeton, NJ: Princeton Books.

Cage. John. *John Cage: An autobiographical statement*. www.newalbion.com/artists/cagej/autobiog.html (accessed January 2004).

Cage, John. 1995. *Cage: Music for Merce Cunningham, volume 4*. Mode. (Compact disc.)

Capote, Truman. 1948. Other Voices, Other Rooms. New York: Random House.

Celichowska, Renata. 2000. *The Erick Hawkins modern dance technique*. Highstown, NJ: Princeton Books.

Cohen, Selma Jeanne, ed. 1998. *International encyclopedia of dance: A project of dance perspectives*. New York: Oxford University Press.

Cohen, Selma Jeanne, ed. 1966. *The modern dance: Seven statements of belief*. Connecticut: Wesleyan University Press.

Cornell, Katherine. February 2001. Canadian warming trend. *Dance spirit*. p. 106-124.

Cornell Chronicle. 1998. Jennifer Tipton to lecture. www.news.cornell.edu/Chronicle/98/10.29.98/Tipton.html (accessed January 2004).

Costa, Arthur L., and Bena Kallick. 2000. *Integrating and sustaining habits of mind*. Alexandria, VA: ASCD.

Curry, Micquelle. Roots and wings. www.alumni.utah.edu/continuum/spring97/vdt.html (accessed January 2004).

Daly, Ann. 1995. *Done into dance: Isadora Duncan in America*. Indianapolis: Indiana University Press.

Demaline, Jackie. March 21, 2003. Julie Taymor enthrones "The Lion King." *The Cincinnati Enquirer*. www.cincinnati.com/freetime/weekend/032103_lionking.html (accessed January 2004).

Dornhelm, Robert, and Earle Mack, directors. 1977. *The children of Theatre Street*. (Video.) Hightstown, NJ: Princeton Books.

Dowd, Irene. *Taking root to fly: Articles on functional anatomy*, 3rd edition. New York: Irene Dowd.

Duncan, Isadora. 1927. *My life.* New York/London: Liveright.

Earthart Drums. Drum making. www.earthart.co.2a/drums.htm (accessed January 2004).

Elia, Susan. 2000. Simonson says. *Dance Teacher*, Vol. 22, no. 10.

Emery, Lynne Fauley. 1988. *Black dance from 1619 to today.* Princeton, NJ: Princeton Books.

Evans, Bill. Bill Evans bio. www.billevansdance.org/bio.htm (accessed January 2004).

Frank, Rusty E. 1990. *Tap! The greatest tap dancers and their stories 1900-1955.* New York: William Morrow.

Franklin, Eric. 1996a. *Dance imagery for technique and performance.* Champaign, IL: Human Kinetics.

Franklin, Eric. 1996b. *Dynamic alignment through imagery.* Champaign, IL: Human Kinetics.

Frich, Elisabeth. 1983. *The Matt Mattox book of jazz dance.* New York: Sterling.

Gardner, H. 1983. *Frames of mind: The theory of multiple intelligences.* New York: Basic Books.

Gardner, Howard. 1999. *The disciplined mind: What all students should understand.* New York: Simon & Schuster.

Gardner, Howard. 1999. *Intelligence reframed: Multiple intelligences for the 21st century.* New York: Basic Books.

Givens, David B. 2004. *The nonverbal dictionary of gestures, signs, and body language cues.* Spokane, WA: Center for Nonverbal Studies Press.

Gold, Rhee. In press. *The complete guide to teaching dance: An insider's secrets to personal and financial success.* Norton, MA: Gold Standard Publishing Company.

Gray, Henry. 1977. *Gray's anatomy of the human body.* New York: Bounty.

Hackney, Peggy. 2002. *Making connections: Total body integration through Bartenieff Fundamentals.* New York: Routledge.

Hamilton, Linda H. 2002. *Advice for dancers: Emotional counsel and practical strategies.* Europe: John Wiley and Sons.

Hanna, Judith Lynne. July 2003. The language of dance from the Kennedy Center ArtsEdge. www.artsedge.kennedy-center.org/professional_resources/overviews/detail.cfm?pub_id=57 (accessed January 2004).

Hawkins, Alma M. 1988. *Creating through dance.* Princeton, NJ: Princeton Books.

Hope's Highland Dancers. Seann Tribuhas (Old Trousers). www.highlanddancer.com/thedances.htm (accessed January 2004).

Horn, Barbara Lee. 1992. *Joseph Papp: A bio-bibliography.* Westport, CT: Greenwood.

Hunter, M. 1982. *Mastery teaching.* El Segundo, CA: T.I.P. Publications.

Isamu Noguchi Garden Museum. People: Martha Graham. www.noguchi.org/graham.html (accessed January 2004).

Johnson, Anne E. 1999. *Jazz tap: From African drums to American feet.* New York: Rosen.

Kenrick, John. 2000, 2003. Making a Broadway musical: Key players: The production team. www.musicals101.com/make1b.htm (accessed January 2004).

King, Alonzo. www.danceadvance.org/03archives/alonzoking2/page08.html (accessed January 2004).

Korean News Service. Famous dance *Snow Falls.* www.kcna.co.jp/item/2002/200202/news02/27.htm (accessed January 2004).

Korn, Mitchell. Artsvision: America's arts education leader (home page). Mitchell Korn bio on www.artsvision.com/biomk.html (accessed January 2004).

Kreigel, M.A., Lorraine Person, and Francis James Roach. 1997. *Luigi's jazz warm up.* Pennington, NJ: Princeton Books.

Kurth, Peter. 2001. *Isadora: A sensational life.* London: Little, Brown.

Ladzekpo, C.K. Foundation course in African drumming. www.cnmat.berkeley.edu~ladzekpo/Foundation.html (accessed January 2004).

Ladzekpo, C.K. C.K. Ladzekpo: Master performer, composer, choreographer, and teacher of African music and dance. http://bmrc.berkeley.edu/people/ladzekpo/Bio.html (accessed January 2004).

Lavender, Larry. 1996. *Dancers talking dance.* Champaign, IL: Human Kinetics.

Lerman, Liz. 1984. *Teaching dance to senior adults.* Springfield, IL: Thomas Press.

Malone, Jacqui. PBS Great Performances biography of Jawole Willa Jo Zollar. www.pbs.org/wnet/freetodance/biographies/zollar.html (accessed January 2004).

McAtee, Robert E. 1993. *Facilitated stretching: PNF stretching made easy*. Champaign, IL: Human Kinetics.

McGreevy-Nichols, Susan, Helene Scheff, and Marty Sprague. In press. *Building dances*. 2nd ed. Champaign, IL: Human Kinetics.

McGreevy-Nichols, Susan, Helene Scheff, and Marty Sprague. 2001. *Building more dances: Blueprints for putting movements together*. Champaign, IL: Human Kinetics.

McGreevy-Nichols, Susan, and Helene Scheff. 1995. *Building dances: A guide to putting movements together*. Champaign, IL: Human Kinetics.

McMahon, Patricia. 2000. *Dancing wheels*. Boston: Houghton Mifflin.

Minnesota News Photographers Association. Mold contamination. www.mnpa.org/poy/2001/package/first/a.html (accessed January 2004).

Mussorgsky, Modest: Pictures at an exhibition. 1992. Produced and directed by Bernar Hébert. Choreographed by Moses Pendleton. Running time 66.12 min. Decca Record Company Limited. Videocassette. London, England and Rhombus Media, Inc.

New York City Ballet. George Balanchine bio. www.nycballet.com/about/nycbgbbio.html (accessed January 2004).

New York City Public Library. Jerome Robbins Dance Division: About the Dance Division. http://nypl.org/research/lpa/dan/danabout.html (accessed January 2004).

Norbury, Alistair, Suzette Newman, Bill Bachle, and Christopher Ramsey. 2001. *The New York City ballet workout*. Video and DVD. New York: Ryko Distribution.

Parsons, David. 1992. *Behind the scenes with David Parsons*. Video format. Patterns. Learning designs and Thirteen/WNET, NYC. Running time 30 mins.

Penrod, James and Plastino, Janice Gudde. In press. *A dancer prepares*. 5th ed. St. Louis: McGraw-Hill.

Public Broadcasting Service American Masters series. Gene Kelly: Anatomy of a dancer. www.pbs.org/wnet/americanmasters/database/kelly_g.html (accessed January 2004).

Quinn, Elizabeth. Overtraining syndrome. Sports Medicine Online. http://sportsmedicine.about.com/library/weekly/aa040600.htm?terms=overtraining (accessed January 2004).

Rudolph, Amelia. Project Bandaloop. www.projectbandaloop.org/mission.html (accessed January 2004).

Schrader, Constance A. 1996. *A sense of dance: Exploring your movement potential*. Champaign, IL: Human Kinetics.

Schwartzman Public Relations. Kenny Ortega press release. www.schwartzmanpr.com/agency/kennyortega.asp (accessed January 2004).

Sousa, David A. 2001. *How the brain learns*. 2nd ed. Thousand Oaks, CA: Corwin Press.

Sullivan, Kathryn. December 2000. Extenuating circumstances: Teaching students how to work with hyperextended knees can help avoid injury and improve technique. www.dance-teacher.com/backissues/dec00/dancehealthy.shtml (accessed January 2004).

Synagogue 2000. Liz Lerman bio. www.s2k.org/Bios/Fellows/lerman.html (accessed January 2004).

The-ballet.com. Ballet training techniques. www.the-ballet.com/techniques/php (accessed January 2004).

The Theatre Museum. Merce Cunningham. http://theatremuseum.vam.ac.uk/placecunn.htm (accessed January 2004).

Thirteen/WNET. Egg, the art show: David Parsons. www.pbs.org/wnet/egg/203/caught/index.html (accessed January 2004).

Thornton, Sam. 1971. *A movement perspective of Rudolf Laban*. London: McDonald and Evans.

Thum, P.J. 2002. FredAstaire.net: The RKO era. www.fredastaire.net/biography/rko.htm (accessed January 2004).

Todd, Mabel E. 1937. *The thinking body: A study of the balancing forces of dynamic man*. Hightstown, NJ: Princeton Books.

Who's Who in Musicals. Bio of Joseph Papp. www.musicals101.com/who13.htm (accessed January 2004).

ABOUT THE AUTHORS

Helene Scheff, RDE, has been a dance educator and administrator for 45 years in both the public and private sectors. She is coauthor of *Building Dances: A Guide to Putting Movements Together* (1995) and its second edition (in press), *Building More Dances: Blueprints for Putting Movements Together* (2001), and *Dance About Anything* (in press).

A registered dance educator, Scheff is the founder and executive director of Chance to Dance, an in-school dance program started in 1985 that brings quality dance education to children in grades four through eight.

A graduate of the famed NYC High School of Performing Arts, Scheff is a former Joffrey Ballet dancer. She is a founding member and former president of the Dance Alliance of Rhode Island and has served as vice president of dance for the Eastern District Association of the American

Helene Scheff

Alliance for Health, Physical Education, Recreation and Dance (EDA). She is a board member of the Rhode Island Alliance for Arts Education and the Committee Liaison for UNITY. Scheff is a member of the National Dance Association (NDA) and a charter member of the National Dance Education Organization (NDEO). Helene was named the Rhode Island Association for Health, Physical Education,

Recreation and Dance's (RIAHPERD) Dance Teacher of the Year in 1996 and was honored as an EDA Outstanding Professional in 1996. She received the RIAHPERD President's Honor Award in 1997 and an NDA Presidential Citation in 1998. She was awarded the Dance Alliance of Rhode Island Dance Legacy Award in 2002.

Marty Sprague, MA, is a professional choreographer and performer with more than 29 years of experience in public dance education. She is a dance teacher at the Providence Academy of International Studies and the artistic director of Chance to Dance.

Marty holds a master's degree in dance education

Marty Sprague

from the Teacher's College at Columbia University. She has been a licensed trainer for the National Center for Education and the Economy's Course I, Standards-Based Curriculum—a professional development course for standards-based teaching and learning. She served on the Rhode Island Governor's Task Force for Literacy in the Arts. Marty is a member of the Arabella Project, a dance group exploring the realms of the older dancer.

Marty is coauthor of *Building More Dances: Blueprints for Putting Movements Together* (2001) and *Dance About Anything* (in press). She also served as a consultant to the authors for *Building Dances: A Guide to Putting Movements Together* (1995) and is coauthor of its second edition (in press).

In 1992 Marty was named the Rhode Island Dance Educator of the Year and in 1998 earned an Outstanding Professional Award from Eastern District Association (EDA). She is a member

Susan McGreevy-Nichols

of National Dance Association (NDA) and a charter member of National Dance Education Organization (NDEO), the Association for Supervision and Curriculum Development.

Susan McGreevy-Nichols is the national director of Arts, Planning and School Support for the Galef Institute in Los Angeles. She taught at Roger Williams Middle School in Providence, Rhode Island, from 1974 to 2002. She was the founder and director of the inner-city school's nationally recognized dance program in which more than 300 of the school's 900 students elected to participate.

Susan is coauthor of *Building Dances: A Guide to Putting Movements Together* (1995) and its second edition (in press), *Building More Dances: Blueprints for Putting Movements Together* (2001), and *Dance About Anything* (in press). She is a charter member and presenter of the National Dance Education Organization (NDEO) and a former treasurer and board member. She also has served as the president of the National Dance Association (NDA) and the nominating chair and (Rhode Island) state leader for the Kennedy Center Alliance for Arts Education.

Susan has received numerous NDA presidential citations and an Eastern District Assciation (EDA) of the American Alliance of Health, Physical Education, Recreation and Dance (AAHPERD) Merit Award in Dance. In 1994 she was named Rhode Island's Dance Teacher of the Year, and in 1995 she was honored both as the NDA National Dance Teacher of the Year and as an EDA Oustanding Professional. She received AAHPERD's Honor Award in 2000.